Plan to Survive I

Plan to Survive I
book 1 of 3
Why, Who, When, and Where: an Overview

By: K.Z. Williams

Book One
Edition 1

Independently Published

ISBN-13: 978-1089521815

This book reviews the results of the author's research and testing. The intent is to guide your survival event response. In no case does the author or publisher take responsibility for results you experience in your application of these guidelines. Needs that must be dealt with in your situation can only be addressed by your modified application of these guidelines.

Express permission from the author is required to copy or in any way disseminate any of the material contained in this book, or available on any associated web site. Guidance obtained from your interpretation of material in this book is not medical or legal advice by the author or the publisher and results solely from the author's research, testing, and observations. Seek the medical opinion of a physician before implementing any portion of the dietary or medical observations in this book. Seek the legal counsel of an attorney before implementing any portion of the regulatory observations made in this book.

DISCLAIMER: The author received or receives no compensation from any manufacturer or other source to recommend or mention any product, service, or source referred to in this book. The author paid for all research and testing; there was no supplier involvement other than shipping.

Foreword

"Finally, a book that overviews this stuff and does not give me information overload. All I want to know is what to expect, what I should do to be ready, and how to deal with possible disasters."

"Being a reviewer on this book gave me the opportunity to think about a subject that I did not understand and to which I had not given much thought. The author purposely asked me to review the book because I was completely unfamiliar with the subject. The author thought I would ask a lot of questions, I did."

"The subject seemed to be so fringe that it was hard to take it seriously. There were subjects that I had not considered. This book answers questions I had overlooked but are important to putting the many facets of this subject into perspective. The book even provides a framework for understanding new information."

"When I stand back and consider what I learned, I realize that just a few precautions copes with most disasters. Even if nothing happens, at least I feel prepared for the unexpected. Given my limited financial resources, it is a great benefit that the book prioritizes supplies for me."

"The news reports an increasing number of disasters. Now is a good time to re-examine this subject. I just wish I had known some of this earlier but as the saying goes, better late than never."

"I am getting a weather alert radio and filtering water pitcher, immediately. I had no idea that the government could use weather alert radios to broadcast disaster messages."

Reviewer comments

Author's Note

Thanks for being interested and reading this book. Being prepared, even at a basic level, gives you an advantage. There is no doubt that some survival event is in our future. Just that its timing is unknown is not a reason to head into it unprepared. I want you to be ready to cope.

I started writing this book 8/2016. It took years to gather and test the information in this book and I want it to get in the hands of people who need to know, now. If you have the time to write a review on Amazon, I **will** take the time to read it, and probably get ideas for the next edition.

Do not waste time. Have at least the top ten survival supplies (Chapter 9) ready for you and your family.

Your opinion matters. It will matter more if people know. Posting an Amazon review will help others. To post a review go to http://www.amazon.com/review/create-review?&asin=B07Y4LMNSM or create one on the Amazon product page review area for *Plan to Survive I*. If you have the time to write a review, I **will** take the time to read it, and probably get ideas for the next edition.

Book two of the *Plan to Survive* series considers details of specific supplies, for advanced preparations you can make for more intense survival events

The pandemic is a warning, of what could happen and why you need to prepare.

Preface

Just how bad is it? In a New Year message UN Secretary-General Antonio Guterres said the world appeared to have gone into reverse before adding, "On New Year's Day I am not issuing an appeal, I am issuing an alert—a red alert for our world."

Russia used cyber-attacks to disable electrical systems, utilities, and financial systems. Other countries, hackers (both for thrills and for profit), and terrorists can too. Without access to electricity and utilities, society would be forced back 100 years. Without a financial system, there would be chaos.

Too often survival books focus on wilderness survival skills. Considering the probabilities of survival events happening, are you more likely to need to know how to survive in your home or in the wilderness? Surviving is more than just knowing how to start a fire; it is an attitude of doing whatever it takes.

Other books often go into excessive detail exploring limited subjects. This book series differs from other books by listing specific supplies for different types of survival events and then describes how to use them. It summarizes major topics and focuses on providing and organizing information to help you get started on a plan to survive.

The benevolent nature of first instincts is to help your community and neighbors when there are problems. **Except** when this first instinct evaporates because an event exists for an extended period and there is no first-responder or third party assistance.

Human instinct is to prioritize self-preservation above all else. Awareness of crisis intensification and escalation can help you prepare for any survival scenario. The intensity of preying on fellow survivors will escalate as survival situations intensify.

Survival scenarios vary in intensity from being inconvenient to major crisis; starting quickly, slowly, or at an elevated level. Being unaware of an escalation compromises your ability to cope:

- **In a normal event**, it might take first-responders 15–19 minutes to reach you.
- **In a survival event**, first-responders will be overwhelmed and may not able to reach you at all.

Be your own first-responder until, and if, trained first-responders are available. Your survival depends on what happens in the first few hours. For instance, a minor fire can grow and threaten your bug-in. Be decisive, act quickly before a minor problem becomes serious.

Desire for normalcy delays or prevents action. Taking action because everyone else is makes you vulnerable to actions directed at masses of people, e.g., the New Orleans Superdome after Hurricane Katrina. Organized mass travel, e.g., evacuation, makes you and your supplies targets. This grouping is not for the benefit of the masses; it benefits those who want to get you to do what they want.

Some of the information in this book is common sense or obvious to readers who have been there, done that. Remember that others will also refer to this book and that they are less knowledgeable than you are. The *Plan to Survive* series can save you time and money by addressing the points you need to consider to survive. Feel free to submit questions at buggingin@gmail.com.

If you would like to know when new books in this series become available, follow me on Amazon's website. Enter *Plan to Survive* or K.Z. Williams in the white search bar at the top of an Amazon web page. Click on the blue (K.Z. Williams) author link of either *Plan to Survive I* or *II*. In the pop-up page that appears, click on the gold color **+Follow** button (left side of page). Amazon will notify you by email when there is a new title available in this book series.

Figure 1. Expect a monumental traffic jam when there is a mass evacuation.

This page intentionally blank.

Contents

This page intentionally blank.

Introduction

Please refer to the Glossary for definitions of terms.

Figure 2. Extreme weather effects

Why Bug-in?

People are becoming aware of and concerned by the frequency of survival situations. If a snowstorm or flood traps you and you are unable to obtain electricity/food/water/gasoline, or a pandemic isolates you, you can survive if you have prepared. Keep in mind that your survival situation will be unique, so plan for that.

Perhaps you need to bug-in due to age, physical, or mental limitations. The *Plan to Survive* series helps you evaluate a bug-in situation and maximize purchasing effectiveness for supplies you need. Survival means accepting hardships. The *Plan to Survive* series reviews supplies and tactics that make it less of a hardship.

Start stocking supplies as soon as you can. Demand for survival supplies is causing prices to rise. Changing weather patterns continue to disrupt global agriculture and make foodstuffs availability less reliable. With a focus on supplying food, labor will divert from manufacturing, which will decrease the availability of other supplies and cause their prices to increase too.

Take time to create checklists. Make a list of supplies you need for each type of survival situation. Then assign responsibilities. Give copies of the list to all members of your survival group. Situations might be sudden or immediate and knowing what to do will result in getting it done faster and with less stress and panic.

You should know how to react to a pandemic, a toxin spill, approaching danger, rioting, or a seismic event. Knowing what to do stops panic and fear. Panic and fear will expose you to life-threatening situations.

Event Types

This book classifies events into five levels: L1 through L5. Each level represents the probability of occurrence, e.g., Super Storm Sandy and Hurricane Katrina were L2 events, verging on L3. There has not been an L5 event in modern history.

Level 1 [L1] = normal (e.g., windstorm or heavy rain)
Level 2 [L2] = severe/extreme (e.g., flooding or hurricane)
Level 3 [L3] = disaster (e.g., pandemic or cyber-attack)
Level 4 [L4] = catastrophe (e.g., EMP or CME)
Level 5 [L5] = The End of the World as We Know It

Realize that any single event type can occur at different intensity levels. For example, a seismic event may become widespread or a local epidemic may become a spreading pandemic. Also, realize that one event may trigger another event, e.g., a seismic event triggering a tsunami, or an asteroid impact on water could create a tsunami that travels on the ocean to strike elsewhere, or a virus mutates and infects survivors of the initial virus.

The probability of any specific event is low. The sum of probabilities is large. Large enough to justify the near certainty of some event happening. Prepare for the most probable events where you live. Your survival situation is unique but there are several possible survival events. Ordering these events by their probability of occurrence yields the priority of your preparations.

cyber-attack	financial crisis
electrical grid failure	pandemic
bio or nuclear attack	tornado or hurricane
super-volcano	seismic activity
tsunami	blizzard or wildfire
violent windstorm	gang violence
terrorist attack	rioting
flooding	fuel or food shortage
social collapse	black hole
gamma ray burst	mini ice age
widespread drought	insect extinction
asteroid impact	EMP or CME

You need to consider whether the situation calls for bugging-in or whether it requires you to bug-out. It is too simple a solution to believe bugging-out is the answer for every survival situation. Bugging-out exposes you to situations that are more dangerous. If you bug-out, you will encounter roving gangs of thugs and risk infections from accidents in unfamiliar surroundings.

When you bug-out the number of items you can bring with you is limited. You must be able to carry them, which is less than you think you can. If you bug-out you may find yourself even more compromised than if you had stayed bugged-in. You will want to take too many supplies with you if you leave a bug-in. Abandon excess supplies while you can.

It is valid to bug-in at first and later decide to bug-out. Chapter 10 focuses on the bug-in or bug-out choice. Survival literature tends to use bugging-out as an all-purpose reaction applicable to all survival situations. Be clear, bugging-in is much less likely to get you killed than bugging-out.

Bugging-out is an overused term and people don't understand the implications. Bugging-out means surviving by competing for limited supplies, which is unlikely to provide you with enough to keep you alive. Gather information about event status and any expected events before you decide to bug-out.

At the end of each chapter in the print version of this book are two blank pages for you to write down and organize your thoughts to decide what is important and what to do.

This is the first book of a series. Book Two, of the *Plan to Survive* series, examines specific example supplies. These examples should help you decide which supplies are the most appropriate for your budget and for events you plan to survive.

Chapter 1
Key Concepts

*Please refer to the Glossary for definitions of terms. The
Introduction explains key concepts used in this book.*

There are two key concepts used in this book. They are
the basis to understand how to control costs when buying,
making, or trading for survival supplies:

> The probability of a survival event decreases as the type
> of event progresses to higher levels of intensity.
>
> Accumulating supplies is additive and enables you to
> survive increasingly intense events.

Cumulative supplies give you a start to survive the next
level event. It reduces expense and time preparing. An
example is storing excess water or food for helping
neighbors in an L2 event. Your survival is paramount.

This effect is why you should focus on lower intensity
events first. Focus on specifics such as:

> where you live
> local response (demonstrated, not verbal assurances)
> how prepared your neighbors are
> how close you are to traffic arteries
> possible radiation leaks
> access to medical supplies
> farming opportunities
> drinkable fresh water

Combining these concepts gives you a powerful tool.
Basic supplies like food, water, and medical supplies are
required. How much to store depends on your anticipation
of intensity, duration, and the size of your survival group.

Survival depends on events for which you accumulate supplies. For example, supplies accumulated for surviving an L3 event are appropriate for an L4 event. An L2 event is probable, an L3 event is realistically possible, an L4 event is realistically possible in your lifetime, and an L5 event is not likely.

Controlling Cost

Controlling cost depends on likelihood of an event. Make location part of a plan. Start your planning with an L2 event. Acquire supplies for surviving L2 events first. Then think about what you need to survive an L3 event. Working on more than one can be overwhelming.

It can get expensive to acquire additional supplies for succeeding levels of events. The good news is that supplies acquired for lower intensity survival events are often useful in lessening effects of more intense events, like having excess water or food.

Acquiring/Storing/Rotating Supplies

Acquiring supplies is a good start. You need to store them and keep them usable. The greatest threat to storing supplies is storage environment. Humidity and temperature extremes or vermin and insect damage can make stored supplies useless. Organic material decomposes, metal oxidizes as rust, plastic becomes brittle, and vermin chew through just about anything. Your best bet is to rotate supplies as they age and to:

isolate them from vermin
use sealed vacuum bags
use desiccants for supplies in sealed bags
use sealed oxygen impermeable storage bins
purge air out of bins before sealing
store supplies at a low temperature and humidity

Keep rotated supplies, like water or food, separate from sealed bins because you need access to rotate them. Even though separate you should keep them grouped in the same area so you can get to them when needed. Drawing a map of storage locations is useful because it helps organize supplies by area.

It is easy to duplicate a supply. Keep cost down by keeping an accurate inventory of stored supplies current. Refer to it before buying a new supply. Print your inventory because there will likely be no or sporadic power. Having more than one storage area is common so have an integrated inventory.

An inventory and a storage area map can locate a supply.

If you keep stored supplies in a cold environment, you are helping to extend their usable storage. Some supplies have a water component that will expand and rupture the container if frozen. Your best bet is to cold store supplies but use a source of heat in extended freezing temperatures if sustained freezing temperatures can damage some of the supplies. Keep a storage area cool and out of sunlight.

Something that meets these criteria is a simple root cellar. The biggest problems are vermin and insects. You should encase the storage bins or the entire storage area in a locking chew-proof enclosure (plastic bins are not chew-proof). Make sure the area drains well; an ideal location would be a hollowed-out hilltop.

Prioritizing Supplies

To help control cost, Book Two of the *Plan to Survive* series classifies survival items into these categories:

A   identifies an item as a necessity to acquire
B   identifies an item as nice to have, but unnecessary
C   identifies an item as unnecessary

Where you live can change your survival planning priorities. For example, if you live in the Rocky Mountain or Northern area you think about cold weather, while living on the East coast biases thinking to hurricanes and ice storms.

In general, think of prioritizing supplies in this order:

1	water
2	food and preparing meals
3	shelter/protection
4	security and self-defense
5	health supplies
6	communications

After working your way through your priority list, start over. You can always use more of everything to make survival more comfortable, or to barter excess for what you need.

In your first pass through a prioritized supplies list, focus on storing only a minimum quantity. Minimum means what is suitable for the size of your group, for whatever you believe the most probable event will be. FEMA often says that this is the quantity needed to sustain each person for 72 hours (three days). FEMA thinks only in terms of the first four line items.

The first four items are the most important, but the next two items become important when event duration is longer than 72 hours. Shelter is important but you can create a temporary shelter. Resist replacing unused stored items with the latest stuff. This rarely provides usefulness that justifies the expense. Book Two of this series focuses on possible items for these general categories.

There are always clever new items. Consider workmanship and reliability before purchasing any. You can purchase an item and look at it more closely at home. If you don't damage it, you should be able to return it. Purchasing and evaluating all alternative products would take too much time and cost too much. Stick to basic functions and decide against items using plastic.

Plastic is not durable. Research a manufacturer. Good customer service is useful when testing to see if a product works as expected. Amazon reviews are a good source of information.

Buy what is necessary to prepare for a specific type of event. Base purchases on expected probability of occurrence and duration. Have enough for the period of survival you anticipate.

L1 events require no purchasing of supplies other than what is ordinary and prudent for a well-stocked pantry. Increase the quantities for longer-term needs. This means that you probably need **at least two weeks** of supplies (per person in your survival group) for an L2 event, and **at least two months** of supplies (per person) to survive an L3 event.

There are supplies unique to L4/L5 events. Supplies you need to survive an L4/L5 event are complex and survivalists have a range of opinions. If you plan to survive an L4/L5 event, you are getting involved in a complex low probability event. Unless you have an unlimited budget, carefully consider whether a product sustains long-term life or just makes it more comfortable.

Preparing for bugged-in survival is a more realistic option than bugging-out. Bug-in survival may be practical for your physical, emotional, or financial state. Bugging-out is an impractical concept for most people. It leads to harmful scenarios, like traveling, having access to supplies while traveling, or having remote supplies stolen. Living at a bug-out location is the ultimate form of bugging-in.

Be aware of the realities of the survival situation. Invest in a weather alert radio and a radio broadcast channel scanner. They let you monitor your area. An analog scanner is cost effective and easier to use than a digital scanner. Having these two devices reduces your need to acquire extra supplies. When you know about available alternatives, you can limit your resupply needs.

Bugging-in effectively means preparing your home with things like exterior lighting. Exterior lighting should use a mix of standard current, photovoltaic (PV) power, or battery powered exterior floodlights and intrusion detection systems. Use a PV system or a generator to power intrusion detection systems when grid power is unavailable.

Consider the probabilities of L1-L5 survival events. Some arguable probabilities of event occurrence are 50% for L1 events, 15% for L2 events, 4% for L3 events, .001% for L4 events, and .0000000001% for L5 events.

Quantification results from subjective considerations. In the end, exact quantification is unimportant. What is important is the probability prioritization and that you prepare for event occurrence based on realizing the diminishing probabilities of more severe survival events.

Level 1 Event

L1 corresponds to daily life in normal circumstances. An L1 event is a short-term disturbance within the L1 period, e.g., severe income reduction or being a hostage. The most probable short-term disturbances will result from cyber-crime and electrical distribution system disruptions.

You can also expect Internet disruptions that limit your Internet activity, e.g. paying bills online. Existing safeguards should limit your exposure.

The severity of an L1 event is under your control if you prepare for the circumstances. An example is that if you are alone and your car breaks down. You can setup a cell phone to record activity and tell anyone offering to help that you are recording the situation and relaying it to a third party. Most L1 events are temporary but some are life threatening. Stay aware of your surroundings and have a concealed weapon when warranted.

Another example is if you experience a reduction in your income. You can use stored supplies to avoid using things that use up limited income. You can even explore chapter 11 bankruptcy for relief. Cyber-mischief makes this likely.

Level 2 Event

L2 events are things like an earthquake, flooding, tornado, or hurricane. Events occur at different intensity and duration. Every area has events that are more probable; focus on those first. Supplies you store need to reflect your expectations and your budget. You must cope with effects of the reaction of the general population and unreliable first responders.

Flooding will be frequent because the air holds more water. There will be heavier rain and snow.

Position yourself to be able to respond to needs without relying on external aid. Often the offer of external aid comes with conditions that require you to follow other rules. Have enough stored food, water, and fuel to avoid exposing yourself to rationing lines and to avoid having rules forced on you.

At this point, you experience the effects of panic in the general population. Panic is not yet severe. You can expect increasing panic among the general population as event severity and duration increase. These will focus on situations where a large number of people gather to claim a limited commodity.

Coping with a large crowd does not mean you need to be obviously armed. Obvious weapons will attract law enforcement attention. Have a concealed weapon, as allowed by local regulations, but put it in view only if you need to protect yourself. Large crowds often act irrationally. Do not assume consistency.

Law enforcement officers do not consider the need to claim a commodity as enough of a reason even to have a weapon. The existence of law enforcement is enough to persuade most people to act rationally. Because there are always occasions when someone or some group becomes irrational, react by abandoning what they want. When you know that you have the commodity stockpiled, there is no need to take an unnecessary risk.

Level 3 Event

L3 events are events like massive tsunamis or pandemics. Most fatalities result from event aftermath. Examples of things that can happen are, encountering water where it is not where it is expected, or there is a lack of adequate medical access, making minor injuries fatal.

Be prepared to provide emergency services. Help contain a situation until professional expertise is available. An example is responding to a fire by containing it with stored fire extinguishers (or wet blankets). After containment, relieve pain and suffering of burn victims. **At a minimum, obtain the basic supplies now**.

At this point, hysteria and panic grows and hinders attempts to help. Just the act of attempting to help will focus attention on you. At times, it will be unwelcome attention. Stay aware of what is happening around you. It could affect your attempt to help in unexpected ways, e.g., attacking you to take medical supplies.

As L3 events get more intense or have longer lasting effects you can expect unreliable or non-existent utilities and services. Sudden unavailability will only amplify general population panic. Panic increases the value of your stored supplies. It also makes your stored supplies a more tempting target for looting.

You need to limit third-party knowledge about what you have and where it is stored. **Don't change this attitude even if you believe the situation is improving. Start maintaining minimal knowledge of the extent, or even existence, of your supplies.** Expect pressure to share your supplies, if others know they exist.

The first priority is your own health and safety. You will not be able to help if you are incapacitated. Being incapacitated includes being infectious. This idea also applies to situations when the actions of an irrational general population prevent helping. Expect fighting over medical supplies if you are dealing with a pandemic.

Level 4 Event

L4 events correspond to things like a massive CME or a super-volcano. In both cases, effects grow more severe and multiply over time, resulting in a complete breakdown of services that organized society depends on. Preparing for events of this intensity means not only immediate survival but aftermath survival too. You will need additional supplies to make it more likely that you survive aftermath effects.

Few people have the time and resources to implement a full plan. Concentrate your first efforts on immediately stocking basic supplies (see Chapter 9). Basic supplies are common to all events and ensure your survival while you scavenge and forage for additional supplies. Use the thought that purchasing the basics now will buy time to make or look for bargains for what you still need. **At a minimum, obtain basic supplies now**.

At this point, it is critical to establish a mutually supporting community of other survivors. Shared supplies and skills will make it possible to successfully deal with unexpected situations. It is impossible (and very expensive) to store supplies that allow you to cope with all the possible situations.

Shared labor is important but having a good mix of skills is more important. Identify the critical skills you need to rely on and try to include group members that have those skills, e.g. medical, dental, firefighting, mechanical repair, combat training. The list of necessary skills is endless. Good intentions from unskilled group members will cause more problems.

Your best bet is to identify a mutual support group, right now. It should come together if an L4 event occurs or if the event is a borderline L3/L4. The labor required to survive an extreme L3 or L4 event will be intense. Having a mutual support group will increase the value of your stored supplies since they would be part of a group response to problems you must cope with.

Level 5 Event

L5 events correspond to events like a gamma-ray burst, a black hole or a pandemic caused by a space borne pathogen. Most events at t-his level end life, as we know it. Some L5 events are survivable but only because of extreme good luck. L5 events are extraordinarily overwhelming but luckily, they are improbable.

In an L5 event, you have total access to all of society's surviving materials. Beware of other survivors who will want what you have. Stephen Hawking, the late brilliant cosmologist, expressed the ultimate survival thought. He thought that humanity needed to spread its population to other planets.

In most L5 events, there will be few survivors. It is impossible to forecast what to expect since an L5 event ranges from cosmological to space borne virus to massive super-volcano eruption. In some cases, there will be no planet left. In other cases, the human race is extinct.

If there is human life left, survival will be grim. Be prepared mentally and emotionally to join with other survivors. You will face a life much like what frontier pioneers faced. Expect ceaseless hard physical labor and subsistence living.

There are L5 event variations you need to consider. They result from our limited knowledge of possible end-effects. A good example is the climate effects we are experiencing. They will only get extreme and intensify if root causes continue to build. Your best bet it to avoid them by relocating.

The planet has experienced climate change before. The point at which climate stabilizes may not support life as we want to live it. Any stabilization point is far in the future. We should be able to force a stabilization point of our choosing. The problem is that people get accustomed to changes, as the new normal.

The worst case is that one event may trigger the occurrence of an even worse event, e.g., a global drought triggers a nuclear exchange as one country tries to grab the remaining resources of a neighboring country. Think of how Iraq tried to take the oil resources of Kuwait to relieve its problems after its war with Iran. The resulting military effort to contain Iraq's aggression almost resulted in a global conflict; some would say it did.

This book tries to provide realistic examples of effects of various types of events. The truth is that events will happen at varying levels of intensity and duration. This will trigger results that become apparent only in the aftermath.

Feel free to modify characterization of any event in this book to meet the events more common to your location. Prepare accordingly but please share your insights by emailing them to buggingin@gmail.com.

Don't feel overwhelmed. There is detailed information available on the web or in the other books in this *Plan to Survive* series. If you have questions or need consulting time, use the email address buggingin@gmail.com.

You will receive a response to all questions. Response time might increase at times due to time constraints. A response depends on question complexity and if the question implies a need for private consulting.

Your opinion matters. It will matter more if people know. Posting an Amazon review will help others. To post a review go to http://www.amazon.com/review/create-review?&asin=B07Y4LMNSM or create one on the book's Amazon *Plan to Survive I* product page review area. If you have the time to write a review, I **will** take the time to read it, and probably get ideas for the next edition.

Referring to an eBook during a survival event requires a charged reader. Will there be electricity?

Notes: Key Concepts

Notes: Key Concepts

Chapter 2
Why You Need Plans

This chapter breaks down and characterizes events that you may need to cope with. Any survival event can take place at varying levels of intensity. This means that any event can escalate to higher and more intense levels. This chapter uses the five levels of events defined earlier to provide a planning framework.

L1 (normal with limited events) > L2 (severe/extreme) > L3 (disaster) > L4 (catastrophe) > L5 (TEOTWAWKI)

Level 1 Event

A Level 1 [L1] survival situation is everyday life. There are personalized L1 events to prepare for. Survival situations could arise because of things such as:

- losing your job
- low level cyber-mischief
- identity theft
- deletion/lock-out of bank account or credit cards
- changing the operation of your car
- terrorism

Cyber-mischief is a likely scenario. Its intent can be either to cause problems for the public sector or for governmental and military operations. Given the recent data breaches and sale of information on the dark web, the problem can only get worse.

Have cash and an old car (pre-1984) available, because it does not use susceptible electronics. You can keep insurance active on an old car by downgrading it to comprehensive and towing. Activate the full policy by calling your agent. You can always use the cash as a type of reserve that you deposit if you need it.

L1 Probability? The probability of normal L1 everyday life occurring is 100%. An arbitrary probability of a temporary major disturbance to L1 everyday life is around 50%.

Level 2 Event

A Level 2 [L2] survival situation usually focuses on extreme or severe weather, minor seismic events, or even minor rioting. Such an event should be relatively brief and temporary. Examples could be an ice storm, contaminated water, high winds, flooding, or services interruption.

You can be relatively sure there will be external aid to help you. It will take time for aid to be effective. Plan to survive on your stored supplies until external aid is effective. Stay aware of possible escalation to an L3 event if the situation persists.

An absolute must to purchase is a weather alert radio with battery backup operation. You should not depend on local broadcasting or a working electrical grid. A useful strategy is to have a unit like the one pictured in Figure 3. The unit in Figure 3 uses three AA batteries for emergency power, i.e., when electricity fails.

Figure 3. Midland WR120/WR120EZ NOAA Weather Alert All Hazard Public Alert Certified Radio with SAME

Specific Area Message Encoding (SAME) technology allows National Ocean and Atmospheric Administration (NOAA) weather warnings specific to your area, or even public safety messages. If forced to bug-out, be sure that one of this type of unit is in each BOB, for use by your survival group.

A caution is that when there is electrical grid failure, the lack of electricity causes an initial limitation of SAME broadcasts. Operators of the SAME system consider local power utility bulletins that project probable system restoration timing. The problem is that the local utility may not be giving a realistic estimate, which causes delay for accurate SAME information.

L2 Probability? An estimated probability of an L2 event occurring is 15% but the probability varies greatly depending on where you live.

Level 3 Event

A Level 3 [L3] survival situation (a disaster) often focuses effects on a geographically limited region. For example, an earthquake is usually limited to a specific region. As L3 event intensity increases, the region it affects gets larger. There are many types of events:

blizzards	flooding
hurricanes	tornados
wildfires	systems failures
political instability	food shortages
financial disruptions	cyber disruptions
cyber-mischief	fuel shortages

An L3 situation is not brief. It has lasting effects that can intensify into severe L3 events. Aid will help you cope with long-term effects but it will take time for aid to be effective and deal with infrastructure damage. If the event if widespread then there may be no aid for a long time. Plan to survive on your own until there is effective aid.

Don't expect to face major looting at first. Depending on event progression, looting will increase. Survivors not as ready as you could resort to violence to take supplies they believe you have.

Do nothing that reveals your survival planning, or that you have supplies, now or later. This includes not traveling outside your home and not looking too clean or too well fed. Minimize third-party knowledge of your supplies before a survival event happens. Starting later is often too late to be effective. Once people are aware of your supplies, they know you as being prepared.

If the L3 event persists or intensifies, you might decide to relocate. Urban areas will become untenable. It is a great temptation to take too many supplies with you. Taking too many supplies could compromise your ability to travel. If you decide to go to a relocation site, getting there will be difficult if you wait too long to make the trip.

Expect gridlocked highways and back roads. Secure supplies at the site and hidden along your planned route. You don't want to appear to have supplies that looters might attack you to get. If stripped of supplies along the way, use supplies you hid along the route. The problem is that you may need to change your route.

Bug-in (shelter-in-place) as long as you can before deciding to relocate. Listening to your All Hazards Weather Alert radio will help you choose a safe area. It needs to be safer than the one where you are. Be aware that many people may attempt to relocate, probably in waves as the information emerges.

You need to stay informed about the evolving state of any survival event, in any location. Any event may trigger other damage, with little warning. Take rioting for instance, it can very quickly move from localized to regional to national to global. Another example is that Hurricane Katrina severe rain caused levees around New Orleans to fail with little warning.

A scanner can monitor police and emergency activity. It acts as a early warning system. Emergency responders know scanners pickup their transmissions so they encrypt them. However, the smallest amount of advance information gives you advantage. The Uniden BC365CRS is an inexpensive analog scanner that has emergency weather alert monitoring too.

L3 Probability? An estimated probability of an L3 event occurring is 4%. It may be increasingly probable as the effects of changing weather patterns become more pronounced.

Level 4 Event

A Level 4 [L4] survival situation (catastrophe) focuses on things such as:

virulent pandemic	electrical grid failure
social collapse	space pathogen
massive tsunami	radiation
EMP attack	biological attack

L3 event effects are typically regional but L4 event effects are national or global. There probably will be limited or no external aid to help you cope with L4 event effects. **You should be ready to survive independently for at least two months.**

L4 catastrophe events tend to focus on massive events. People (or governments) could be the cause of L4 catastrophes. It is entirely possible that manmade L4 events will have built in safeguards to prevent the event from getting out of control. Stay aware of escalation. If the event persists, assess whether a war is likely and whether it could magnify the effects.

In the near-term, this planet will experience warmer temperatures. Although this planet has experienced periods of warm/hot temperatures before, there was not a human population. In addition to frequent extreme weather, there will be crop failures and food shortages but this leads to long-term effects.

The most likely long-term effect is a new ice age. Ironically, it results from a rising temperature. Rising temperature disrupts the North Atlantic circulation system (specifically the Gulf Stream). The Gulf Stream brings warm South Atlantic water to the North Atlantic. Fresh water from the melting Greenland ice cap is disrupting this circulation. This disruption will eventually cause colder temperatures in the northern hemisphere.

Colder temperatures will cause temperature drops in North America and even more so in Great Britain and Europe. The Gulf Stream may stabilize away from the fresh water run-off. If it does not, then relocate to avoid the initial effects (mostly agricultural and transportation disruption, along with weather disruption).

It may take years for Gulf Stream disruption to stabilize. Even if it stabilizes, there will be a new normal. This makes it an event that you can start to plan to survive but you have time to get ready for it.

Starting with L4 catastrophes, think about leaving a bug-in location and moving to a location distant from the L4 event. In other words, start-out planning to survive in your home but at some point, decide to relocate. You have time to choose what supplies to take. Some probable L3/L4 U.S. events are:

Cascadian subduction zone rupture (and tsunami)
San Andreas fault earthquake (It is the above sea level continuation of the Cascadian subduction zone; an event in one may trigger an event in the other.)
New Madrid fault earthquake
East coast –ice, flooding, hurricanes, storm surge
West coast –forest fires, earthquakes
Gulf coast – rainstorms, hurricanes, and storm surge
Northern –cold (and getting worse), blizzards, flooding
Midwest – flooding, blizzards
Southern – tornadoes, heat, humidity, flooding
Plains – tornadoes, blizzards, flooding
Rocky Mountains – blizzards, forest fires, snow melt flooding
Northwest – forest fires
Southwest – heat, flash floods, forest fires

An event in one of these areas could easily intensify due to additional weather effects and ensuing situations. For example, a blizzard or rainstorm can become an ice storm, knocking out electrical power and making a trip to the grocery store impossible. Some events may require bugging-out at once due to immediate effects, e.g., floods, tsunamis, wildfires, or earthquakes.

L4 Probability? An estimated probability of an L4 event occurring is .001%.

Level 5 Event

A Level 5 [L5] survival situation (TEOTWAWKI) is massive and global. It focuses on things like a black hole, large asteroid impact, massive CME, super-volcano, or a gamma ray burst. L5. TEOTWAWKI events require extensive preparations for situations that affect all facets of life, directly or indirectly.

Surviving L5 events will be terrifying. If a large asteroid hits the planet, there can be varying effects that depend on composition. A grazing gamma ray burst event is survivable but not a direct strike. A black hole event may not be survivable at all. There is a theory that very small black holes pass through the planet often.

There will be no external aid to help you cope with the effects of an L5 event, if you survive it. Surviving it involves a large amount of luck. Preparing may be a futile exercise. Survivalists go to great lengths to prepare for this type of event, even though the probability of it is extremely small (but not zero). Given the great expense, it is difficult to recommend pursuing this preparation level.

You can too but the planning it takes is intricate. Survivalists lead lives dedicated to surviving unlikely L5 events. They share tips on how to stretch their financial resources so they can maximize their preparations. Their lifestyle is unique and usually leads to mutual support because the lifestyle is difficult to understand.

L5 Probability? An estimated probability of an L5 event is around .000000001%, small but not zero.

Sample Event Scenarios

Maybe you are confused about how to compare survival events to the L1/L2/L3/L4/L5 framework used in this book. The main cause of confusion is the wide range of possible events. A hypothetical example of each type of event type may help you.

In an L1 event you may have a bad flu that keeps you from working for a couple of weeks and you have no income.
In an L2 event, there is regional widespread flu (an epidemic). Commerce and utilities are affected.

In an L3 event, there is national then global flu. Commerce is highly limited, including food/fuel distribution and utilities. Medical science eventually develops a vaccine.

In an L4 event, melting permafrost releases a pathogen that takes months to achieve medical control. During that time, there is no global commerce and no utilities or services.

In an L5 event, a space borne virulent pathogen reaches Earth and uses chemistry unknown to medical science. No reliable vaccine or cure ever exists.

These examples show how an event can intensify. They also show how easy it is to misunderstand the seriousness of a situation. A delayed understanding slows the response. Delays often result from waiting until it has intensified and is more difficult to control.

No level of supplies advance preparation can take the place of knowing what to do, how to do it and when to do it. Surviving an L3/L4/L5 event gets increasingly difficult if you don't have the skills to cope.

This page intentionally blank.

Notes: Why You Need Plans

Notes: Why You Need Plans

Chapter 3
Who Will Survive?

Who survives depends on having pre-determined plans ready to put into action. When an event occurs, there is too stress, anxiety, fear, and panic. They prevent rational and timely response.

There will be an immediate and growing need for people to carry out their pre-planned reactions. Planned reactions ensure survival. Creating a set of plans makes precise reaction automatic.

One plan .the need for security guards, gives you time to activate other plans. **Implement this plan first**. Guards prevent stealing or equipment damage. Survival plans depend on knowing where specific supplies are.

Strength in Numbers

You will need to provide for a growing number of tasks such as:

guard/patrol duty	preparing food
inventory control	communications
laundry	foraging
maintenance	hunting and fishing
water gathering	firewood gathering
bartering	medical assistance
hygiene monitoring	shelter maintenance

How do you get the time, especially when tasks need to be performed simultaneously? You need other survivors to work with. Having supplies makes you attractive to other survivors.

The best plan for coping with an L3/L4, or even L5 event, includes forming or identifying a survival group before an event happens. If you are not a member of a group when an event has happened, you can test your compatibility with a newly formed group. Have your supplies remote from the group and bring supplies to them on an as needed basis to see how they react.

If you have a list of supplies you have stored, you can show this list to a group as a way of gaining acceptance. Beware that if you show the list to the wrong group they might kill or abandon you after finding out where your supplies are located.

The larger your group is the more likely that it will be the focus of people that want to "share" your resources. They must find you first. Always assume someone is watching you and hide your movements, even at your bug-in location. Avoid being followed by wearing non-descript, dirty and ragged clothes and constantly looking behind and around you. Use indirect travel to get home.

Long-term Consequences

Expect massive die-offs in the general population. This will be a terrible reality if survival circumstances last longer than a week, with no external sources of food and water or medical attention. People will do desperate things and will try to take whatever supplies from you they think they need to stay alive. Keep a low profile and let the population decrease so there will be less danger to your ability to survive; it may take two or three months.

This will be a dangerous and stressful period so don't do anything sudden or rash. One of the worst mistakes you can make is to use up your supplies based on the thought that rescue is imminent. Even if there is a verbal promise of aid, don't use up your supplies expecting the aid to show up. Circumstances often change and the aid may never appear.

In general, you want to blend-in with other survivors. Look thin and gaunt when away from your bug-in. Disguise your appearance with baggy dirty clothes and with hooded sweatshirts. Hide your clean hair and well-fed face; even your shoes should look scuffed, ragged, and dirty. Keep all supplies out of sight because you don't know who is watching, and might think that if you have one supply you might have others.

Be prepared for emotional appeals for help. As calloused as this may sound, realize that your first priority is your own survival. If you can't say no, have a supply of "go away" kits to hand out. These kits should not advertise how well you are prepared because word will spread to other survivors.

There is always a need for compassion. There will be times when you need to decide what the right thing to do is. You never know when an act of compassion will result in help when you need it. Customize your "go away" kits (see prior paragraph) for limited specific needs.

Use supplies your group has as effectively as possible. Usually this means using your judgment about what is necessary. These are a series of possible action plans to help you use supplies effectively. Please modify them to fit your needs.

Energy Plan (Non-electrical)

The energy plan focuses on minimizing use of non-replenishable fuel. Use replenishable fuel like wood or coal as much as you can. You might choose not to use some fuel sources since there are fumes, odors, and smoke that can give away your position or your supplies status. Propane and electricity are the only common energy sources that are odorless and smokeless.

You can store propane indefinitely but storing it is dangerous. Propane is heavier than air; if it leaks, it will collect in pockets in storage area depressions. These pockets are extremely dangerous because propane does not immediately dissipate. For this reason, never store propane in any structure where an ignition source can cause a pocket to explode.

There will be survivors scavenging for wood. Do not scavenge wood that is treated, stained, or painted. Stockpile it so you can have a fire when it is limited. Replenish it as you use it; gather wood as you find it.

All wood burns at the same level of heat but soft woods, leave more ash and burn rapidly.

You will need to use gasoline-powered equipment. You should store gasoline. Gasoline is a blend of unstable highly refined substances. Safe gasoline storage depends on several factors. Store stabilized gas in plastic cans in a pit to control storage temperature and for safety. Survival plans often depend on a gasoline-powered generator and a gasoline-powered car. Diesel fuel is a better choice but equipment is costly and hard to find.

Electrical Plan

An electrical plan should use both small batteries and at least two different types of electricity generation systems. The easiest generation system to obtain and maintain is a gasoline powered portable generator.

Our lives depend on having electricity but you can live without it. It is almost impossible to survive any event without having at least a limited amount available. A car battery is an alternative electrical source, when attached to an inverter. When electricity is not available, survivors will desperately look for other sources.

Some inverters are so large and draw so much current that they need direct connection to a car battery. Some are so large that they draw enough current to blow a car fuse or melt its wiring.

Small batteries can be rechargeable or non-rechargeable. Alkaline batteries are a common non-rechargeable type. Nickel metal hydride (NiMH) is a common rechargeable type. There are rechargeable types for specialized purposes, lithium-ion and nickel cadmium (NiCad).

Rechargeable small batteries cost more than non-rechargeable alkaline batteries. Charging and reusing rechargeable batteries lowers the unit cost of the cumulative amount of power used. Eventually their unit cost of power is less than the unit cost of power supplied by disposable alkaline batteries.

There are downsides to rechargeable batteries. The amount of time they hold a charge is less than that of alkaline batteries. They have a shorter shelf life (from 3-5 years, based on brand). Shelf life varies based on storage temperature. NiMH batteries store for about four years and can hold almost a full charge at the end of year three. They still work after being stored for five years but rapidly lose charge capacity after year three.

Lithium-ion battery output is at a higher voltage (useful for night vision equipment) but lose about 18% of their capacity per year. Some LED flashlights have greater intensity light when powered by lithium-ion batteries because of the higher voltage.

Alkaline batteries often advertise a 3-5 year shelf life (enough for frequent use). Higher cost alkaline batteries advertise a 10-year shelf life (good for storing). Batteries expire when stored charge degrades to 80% of maximum, but they are still usable.

It might appear that you should use rechargeable NiMH batteries but that may not be true. If you store batteries (and do not rotate them frequently enough) then alkaline batteries become more cost effective. Depending on your willingness to absorb cost you should choose between rechargeable NiMH and alkaline. Rotate all batteries by replacing them with new ones periodically.

If you store rechargeable NiMH batteries for a long period, they may be unusable when needed. If you store NiMH batteries, you should periodically check them with a recharger/tester like the LaCrosse rechargeable battery tester. When stored charge capacity declines 20% consider replacing the batteries.

Lithium-ion LED flashlights have greater light intensity. Night vision equipment often uses lithium-ion powered IR illumination. Store a few lithium-ion batteries for these specific uses. Lithium-ion batteries are expensive and lose charge capacity over time. You might want to limit the number of devices that use them.

Use NiMH batteries in non-critical devices but replace them every five years. Use rechargeable lithium-ion batteries in a limited number of critical devices and replace them every five years. Use non-rechargeable alkaline batteries in non-critical devices and replace them every three to ten years, or as needed.

Do not use sharp objects to remove rechargeable batteries after charging. The batteries often have fragile electronic chips.

You can learn to live without electricity but it takes time. In that time, you will need electricity. It was difficult to decide whether to include the following basic information. It is here because not including it would be a disservice to you if this is the only book of the *Plan to Survive* series that you read (Book Two includes more information).

A common generator measurement is a watt. One thousand watts is a kilowatt (KW). The more powerful (and more expensive) a generator is, the greater the KW rating. A generator that generates 5,000 watts of continuous power and surge power of 6,250 watts is adequate for normal loads, not for powering a house.

Selecting a generator

Remember two things when selecting a generator:

> The surge rating is for a very short period. Using it for more than a fraction of a second may destroy a generator.
>
> An overload can destroy the generator; 75% of the rated running output is usually an optimum generator load.

A caution is that most generators have an automatic shut-off when the oil level is low. When you test run your generator (every two years) check the oil level. It is possible to by-pass an automatic shut-off for low oil level.

There are generator alternatives to choose from. A key decision is whether it should be portable, which it should be. Size its power need conservatively:

> Estimate your running electrical load. Consider what loads need power, when they need it, and how long they will use it. Use something like a Kill-A-Watt metering device to measure the size of electrical loads. Find out the startup power for each. Disconnect unneeded loads.
>
> Determine which generators work for your load. Calculate your survival load as loads that are necessary, not just convenient or for the sake of comfort.
>
> Use a survival load of 75% of running capacity. Be aware of starting requirements for each load and compare total loads to startup power (surge) rating.

In some cases, the startup and running loads will be the same, e.g., TVs, lights, and laptops. In other cases, the starting load will be a greater (3 or 4 times, or more) than a running load. Examples of these types of appliances are; refrigerators, freezers, air-conditioners, microwaves, coffee pots, hair dryers, pumps, drills, saws etc. Don't try to power your home because unexpected loads will destroy the generator.

Decide what fuel you want to use. Think about the fuel source. A dual fuel generator is desirable only if you are certain of fuel availability. Decide if you want it to be a fixed installation or portable. Get an idea of installation costs (it is much more for fixed than for portable).

Buy a generator that meets load requirements and your budget. Install it and get a fuel supply that complies with local laws. If it is portable, make sure you chain the unit down. If it is a fixed unit, have a professional install it and connect it to your load panel.

Running a generator

Prepare to run it. Store fuel or connect a gas pipe. If you use gasoline, remember generators use 8-15 gallons a day. Store stabilized gasoline in a ventilated area where the temperature does not fluctuate (at a lower temperature). Never store gasoline in an enclosed space. Be aware of applicable local regulations.

Natural gas pipelines rely on pumping stations that use electrical compressors. The compressors usually have only a three-day fuel reserve for a backup generator.

If you store and use liquid fuel (e.g., gasoline or propane), practice using a fuel transfer system. It is a good idea to have a backup system because failure of a transfer system can be dangerous.

Store a shelter and an air filtration system because you need to be able to run the generator in all weather, including dust storms. Rain can quickly destroy a generator. Wind can quickly knock down a shelter. Dust has varying effects, based on its composition, structure, and the environment, but the worst case is volcanic dust. If dust enters the engine it will quickly wear out the engine and it will become inoperable.

Purchase extension cords and multi-outlet strips for power distribution and test-run the system so you can identify other components you need. Use heavy-duty extension cords for primary distribution lines. After buying additional distribution components, test the system again.

Run a high amperage electrical supply cord into your home, possibly through the wall. Do it now and cover any outside access gaps so rain and dirt don't get in it. This prevents having an open window or door. **Do not connect it to your house wiring and its load.**

Safely operating a generator

Wear gloves when starting it with a starter rope.

Never run the generator indoors.

Keep the exhaust away from any windows or doors where exhaust fumes can get into your home.

Use a carbon monoxide (CO) detector in your home near where you position a running generator.

Do not overfill the fuel tank. Leave a ½-inch air gap.

Do not fill the fuel tank while it is running; fumes ignite.

Leave space around the generator to avoid building-up heat. A generator that has been running needs to cool.

Filter the air intake if ash or dust is expected. They will destroy the engine. Keep the filter clog free.

A generator is an electrical device so keep it dry or it will stop working. That means keep it out of the rain too.

Maintaining a generator

Test run your generator every two years.
Check the oil before the test-run because most generators have an automatic shutoff for low oil. It may be stuck.
Put two cups of fuel with fuel stabilizer in the tank.
Start it with no load attached. If you want to test with a load, add them one at a time so that the generator is not overloaded. Testing into the surge power will destroy the generator. Use something like a Kill-A-Watt meter to measure load.
Run the generator and let it stop by using up all the fuel.
Close the fuel line valve but leave other controls in the run position, then wrap it for storage. This keeps tank condensation out of the engine.
Store it out of sun, with a cover to protect against debris.
Check the cover periodically for holes (mice and squirrels chew on tarps) because holes let the generator get wet.

Gasoline and diesel-powered generators make noise. Its sound tells people that not only were you prepared but that you might have other supplies. If a survival situation extends for more than two or three weeks you should cease using the generator because of its noise level.

Photovoltaic systems

When stored fuel runs out, use a photovoltaic (PV) or solar array system. A PV system is silent. A downside is that they generate far less power than a generator. Another downside is that the charge controller they use is delicate and connecting it incorrectly destroys it.

If you can afford a geothermal generator, do it. It is odorless, silent, and fuel is almost inexhaustible (water from an aquifer and subterranean heat). However, if there is a seismic event it may not work because drilled pipes may collapse or shear-off. It is not portable.

Larger PV systems use 12-volt batteries to store power for use when the PV panels are not setup or when power use exceeds PV system output. How much power a PV system generates depends on the strength of solar energy (e.g., angle of solar panels, position of sun, shadows, clouds, time of day) and how many PV panels. Things you need to be aware of when using a PV system:

Battery power provides direct current (DC) at a fixed voltage. It is inefficient to use an inverter to transformers that convert AC power back to DC. Use electrical devices that are DC as much as possible. Use devices that plug-in directly to the DC power source, which usually means using automobile cigarette lighter type plugs.
Most inverters tend to be low power (less than 400 watts). Using them will drain a battery bank. Have at least two or three if you must use one. Many inverters have a built-in fan that stays on even when the unit is not in use.
Get one or two higher wattage inverters (at least 500 watts, each) for higher power needs, e.g., using a power tool. Remember that a startup power requirement can be much higher than the running requirement.
It is easy to see a PV system and it is easy to steal. **Protect a PV system at all times.** You could chain a PV system to earth anchors. Consider using only some of your PV panels at any one time so that others are in reserve if the setup is stolen or damaged.
You need to use a charge controller to charge batteries from a PV system. There are two types, pulse wave modulated (PWM) and maximum power point tracking (MPPT). PWM charge controllers are less expensive than MPPT charge controllers are. Use PWM controllers on systems that generate less than 800 watts.
For larger PV systems use a MPPT charge controller. Although mostly silent, the charge controller you use

may have an audible integrated fan. Save the charge controller manual for reference because using it is not obvious.

Connect a charge controller carefully; it is easy to burn out. When setting the system up connect it to the battery first. Disconnect it from the battery last when taking the system down. Have a backup charge controller.

The battery bank of the PV system is an expensive part of a PV system. Use at least two 12-volt deep-cycle batteries with the highest amp-hour rating you can afford. Use a battery maintainer to keep them charged (to float level). Trickle chargers may damage your battery bank because they don't detect over-voltage and don't have over-charging protection.

A car battery primarily starts an engine. Deep-cycle batteries take into account both starting an engine and providing energy for other devices. A car battery could damage electronics by sending an engine-starting surge of electricity.

After about five years, you need to replace the batteries. Deep cycle batteries can last up to 10 years in a controlled low temperature environment. Be aware that all battery capacity degrades over time and that after 10 years of optimum storage any lead-acid battery cannot hold a charge. Fuel cell and lithium-ion battery banks look promising.

Water Plan

The water plan is to have a renewable source. Use it after using all your stored water. You can stay alive short-term by drinking one liter of water a day, surviving long-term means you need to increase water consumption. You can easily increase to two or three liters a day.

Cooking, hygiene, cleaning, washing, etc. can easily take at least a ½ gallon more a day of drinkable water. Try to use recycled (used) water as often as possible but remember that toxins can be absorbed through the skin. For more detail, read Book Two of this *Plan to Survive* series of books, and research alternatives.

For additional drinkable water, use disinfected or filtered surface water. If you use surface water, avoid contamination like lawn or agricultural chemicals. When in doubt, do not drink it. Try to use non-drinkable water for things like flushing the toilet or cleaning non-eating surfaces but don't bath in it. Please refer to Book Two of this *Plan to Survive* series.

Products like Kool-Aid are flavor enhancers for odd tasting filtered water. Children and the elderly are sensitive to odd tasting water.

You can capture 124 gallons of drinkable water from ½ an inch of rain on a 20' x 20' area, subject to legal restrictions. In an obvious survival situation, legal restrictions on rainwater collection are not enforced. Most roofs use shingles that contaminate run-off. Some roofs use metal, which provides drinkable water if you discard the initial run-off.

Use a food-grade piece of plastic sheeting to catch run-off rain. Take advantage of the fact that no land is perfectly flat. Use natural surface drainage to channel water to a corner with a pot in a hole. A small pot may fill quickly. Immediately start transferring water collected in the pot to food grade plastic containers. Remember that water will make the containers heavy. Wait until event airborne chemicals, ash, pathogens… subside.

You can survive on one liter of water per day, if you are inactive. One liter is a minimum. If you are active, you will need more. Your body uses water for perspiration to cool itself. You will need a lot of water if you are active or in hot weather. If you are ill, your body will need extra water to flush out toxins and dead viruses that your kidneys filter out.

Shelter Plan

The shelter/housing and sleeping plan should use your home as the primary shelter. If necessary, set-up a large tent to serve as an alternative shelter. Small tents can be set-up in your house for trapping heat while sleeping. The primary purpose of any shelter is to prevent exposure to weather that could cause hypothermia.

You may find it necessary to setup a temporary shelter. The purpose of a temporary shelter is to set it up quickly as a usable shelter while you work on a more permanent shelter. A temporary shelter must meet immediate needs without using up time better spent pursuing immediate needs.

Hypothermia is the greatest killer in survival situations. Hypothermia starts when your trunk cools to less than 95°F and impairs your ability to think clearly. It is fatal when the trunk gets down to 68°F. You can get it at temperatures above freezing if you cool down too quickly, by either perspiration or getting wet. Hypothermia can set in slowly so watch for its signs.

Keeping warm and dry is critical, especially when sleeping. If you are not, you are probably not alert enough to recognize environmental changes, e.g., when your heating system stops because electricity turns off. You can go into hypothermia and shock if you don't get warm immediately (but slowly).

When you are warm, you can make better decisions as to what needs to happen. To stay warm always have immediate access to a sleeping bag to avoid digging through your emergency supplies to find it. Keep a warm stocking cap with your sleeping bag. Your body may be in the sleeping bag but your head is not. Even when the bag has a hood, there is limited insulation in the hood.

If you are trying to stay warm, realize that space blankets are poor blankets. They trap body moisture and get you damp, which can lead to hypothermia. If you want to reflect heat make sure the shiny side of a space blanket faces the heat source. If you want to trap heat, reverse this orientation. They tear and the metallic coating flakes off if folded or in contact with rough surfaces. They may be poor blankets but they have many other uses.

A use is as shelter coverings when you want to reflect heat from the sun and/or block rain from leaking into your shelter. If you use one to reflect heat during the summer, reverse it in the winter. Tie it down, including the surface, to prevent wind damage. If you use multiple space blankets to cover a shelter, layer them so rain does not leak in at the seams.

Since space blanket packages are small and inexpensive, buy several for spares. Since they trap body moisture, their usefulness as blankets is minimal but they are useful as rain barriers. They don't need to be disposable but if they wear or have bodily fluids on them dispose of them. A good use for a space blanket is to keep injured people from going into shock. Preventing hypothermia-induced shock to injured people is a great use.

Clothing is really a form of portable personal shelter. You can enhance its shelter capability by layering it (for temperature control). A problem is that it alone does not offer sufficient isolation from an inhospitable environment.

Hunting Plan

The hunting plan is not to hunt or fish if you are near

an urban area. If you do hunt or fish, do it only as safe opportunities arise, e.g., being in a rural area. There are many reasons to limit hunting and fishing:

other hunters or fishermen could shoot you
other survivors could take bagged game from you
you might lead others back to your bug-in
you could bag a diseased animal
you use limited ammunition on an unproductive hunt

It is probable that bagged game caloric intake will be insufficient to meet daily needs. If you prepare game incorrectly, you can get sick or make others sick. Hunting and fishing time and effort would be more useful if used for gathering and foraging.

Security/Defense Plan

The security/defense plan uses a continuous day and night guard. There is a high probability you will need to react to other survivors acting irrationally. Maintain layers of detection around your home so you get intrusion warning(s). Don't depend on just one warning system. Looting attacks will happen at night, by people believing they are well armed enough to overpower you.

A layer of protection that is particularly effective is the battery powered motion detection light. Battery powered lights are especially useful because in most survival events the electrical grid will not work. Light that turns on at motion detection will startle intruders. It often scares them off or gives you time to use counter-measures against them, to make them leave.

Consider using solar powered motion lights as backup. Consider using grid powered lighting for large area illumination since electrical grid failure is not common to all events. Having grid powered lighting will condition some looters to expect it and avoid your location.

Another layer of defense blocks approaches to your bug-in or channels intruders into known approaches. Caltrops (sharp multi-angle spikes) block approaches and when thrown behind a moving vehicle disable pursuit. Nail boards block approaches where direct observation is limited or impossible. When attackers wear thick-soled boots, caltrops and nail boards are ineffective.

Nail boards use boards with nails driven completely through a thin piece of wood. Anchor nail-boards to the ground where you place them. Caltrops and nail boards can channel prowlers into paths where other motion detectors are setup. Motion detectors can be anything that lets you know of their presence. A motion detector is something as simple as a trip wire connected to a noisemaker, like gravel in a can.

Having and showing firearms will persuade many looters to go somewhere else, but don't count on it. **Don't trust your life to chance**. Be ready to use firearms when it is necessary. A firearm is useless if it is out of position or not loaded. Preloaded magazines should be pre-positioned for the guard(s), so there is no lapse in activity. Time-outs don't happen in looting attacks.

The start of a firefight may be loud or only sensed as possible. Guard(s) must alert others to load more magazines and be ready to help. **Being wrong is okay. Do not look for a fight.** Avoid one if reasonably possible but recognize that if a fight starts you need to end it decisively, so looters do not come back.

Firearms Plan

Addressing the topic of firearms is a painful exercise. Not only is there an overwhelming amount of hard to digest information but there is a lot of conflicting opinion. The subject is almost a holy war among proponents of varying points of view.

The objective of this book is to give you an actionable plan for firearms. Using these recommendations, you can make a final decision based on your unique needs.

Simplicity is the biggest consideration. A firearm that is complex is hard to use or maintain. The goal of this book is to save you time and money used to research, test, and select a firearm. Keep in mind that firearms are restricted in some places. **Find out what regulations apply before you purchase a firearm**. These are some general guidelines for purchasing firearms for specific uses:

- shotguns and pistols for close defense (up to 50 yards)
- .22-caliber rifle for hunting and close defense (up to 50 yards)
- small rifle, e.g., an AK-47, for intermediate defense (up to 250 yards but 50 to 100 yards is more likely)
- hunting rifle, e.g., a .30-06, for long-distance defense and precision shooting at 400 to 800 yards
- small 9mm pistol for personal defense, concealed carry
- large frame .45 caliber pistol for home defense
- .22-caliber pistol, with a noise suppressor if possible, for urban hunting and pest control

Get a concealed carry permit. Some states allow open carry. Find out what laws apply and comply with them.

There are numerous firearms purchasing alternatives and reasons. The bottom line is that you should use whatever firearm makes you comfortable. Get extra magazines, as allowed by your state, because there may be no time to reload. Choose ammunition carefully, some is unreliable and some use bullets that go through walls. Practice until you know how to use the firearm safely.

Practice getting an unloaded firearm in the most useful position; that also means to practice drawing an unloaded concealed pistol.

You need to be able to watch and guard all approaches. You can be certain looters will use an approach that conceals them. You may be able to disable them while they are hiding. Concealment means that something blocks visibility, while cover means that something not only blocks visibility but also direct fire from a weapon. **You can shoot through concealment if you know your target is there but be sure that only the target is there.**

Edged Weapons Plan

The second most used weapons will be knives and other edged weapons (the first is a club). There are two types of knives, fixed or folding blade. Heavy clothing will often stop a slashing attack but not a stabbing attack. Try to keep exposed skin to a minimum if exposed to a slashing attack. Remember that a moving target is much harder to defeat for both knife and club attacks. Keep moving, even if only shifting your stance.

Fixed blade knives can inflict stabbing wounds to puncture vital organs. Concealed folding knives mostly inflict slashing in fast attacks. Either can inflict a wound that causes the victim to bleed-out. It is difficult to conceal a fixed blade knife, making their presence obvious. A folding knife takes time to draw and deploy.

Other types of edged weapons include machetes, axes, maces, spears, pikes, and tomahawks. Although not concealable, they are deadly when a person has trained to use one. Tomahawks are especially deadly because they can slash like a knife, puncture like a sword, or strike like a club. Having an edged weapon in each hand lets you alternate their use, confusing an attacker.

Don't depend on a knife for self-defense if you don't train with it. Training gives you skills to use it effectively. Training does not need to be extensive but without it an attacker could take your knife and use it on you. In a survival situation, law enforcement officers may arrest you if you openly carry one, no matter what your reason is.

To thwart slashing knife attacks make a kind of tunic from woven Kevlar cloth. These tunics should stop slashing knife attacks and give you time to deal with the threat. You need special shears to cut the cloth before you sew it. It will ruin ordinary scissors. Because it is woven fabric, you can sew it with a sewing machine by using heavy-duty needles (expect to break a few), or by hand. Extra panels of Kevlar hinder stabbing.

Medical Plan

The medical plan uses limited supplies for maximum benefit. The best course of action is to avoid accidents that may lead to life threatening infections. More people die after an event than during it because of inability to treat wounds and to maintain hygiene.

Keep supplies in sealed baggies to limit rain damage or other contamination. Not all baggies are waterproof.

Bacteria and viruses exist in great numbers on your skin and they get into open wounds. Have a portable medical kit ready. Treat all wounds as possible cases of infection because the first hours are critical to medical survival. You should take first-aid courses focused on what to do.

Just having medical supplies may be enough to make a hysterical crowd act irrationally. **Do not advertise medical capability** unless the situation will not endanger you. Your best bet is to keep most of your medical supplies well hidden, even at your bug-in.

A medical kit needs to be portable and comprehensive. Pain and suffering will be all around you and the ability to moderate it will be invaluable. In a survival situation, you need to act quickly and decisively. Your first priority is to take care of yourself and your survival group.

The need for pain and fever relief will be great. Ibuprofen (Advil) is best for relieving pain while acetaminophen (Tylenol) is best for relieving fever. Aspirin is general purpose. Antihistamines can relieve allergic reactions. Include basic health evaluation and monitoring equipment. The monitoring equipment is for patients with complex conditions that you try to relieve.

Purchasing an off-the-shelf first aid kit is not a good idea. They typically use minimal or sub-standard supplies. The supplies do not deal with a variety of injuries. You should assemble your own medical/first-aid kit. Supplementing an off-the-shelf wilderness first-aid kit is a good option.

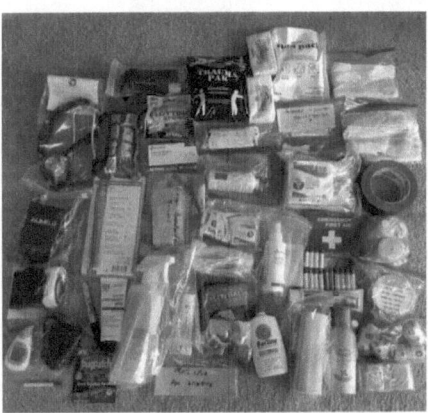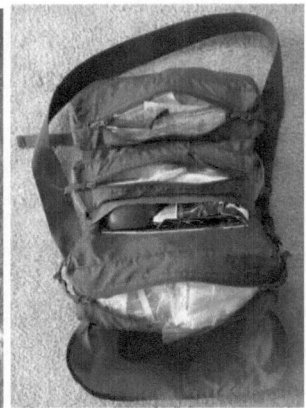

Figure 4. Supplemented medical kit for common problems

This kit contains:

- stethoscope for checking the condition of a patient
- wrist cuff for blood pressure monitoring

- non-invasive temperature measuring device
- blood oxygen content monitor (finger-tip)
- tourniquet for stopping major bleeding
- elastic wraps for sprains and general immobilization
- hemostats for blood vessel bleeding control
- tweezers for removing material from wounds
- topical anesthetic for relieving pain (4% lidocaine)
- burn spray (2% lidocaine)
- flat tin of pills with:
  - ibuprofen (Advil) for major pain relief
  - acetaminophen (Tylenol) for major fever relief
  - aspirin for pain and minor fever relief
  - naproxen sodium (Aleve) for muscle and joint pain
  - loperamide anti-diarrhea pills
  - Benadryl tablets for minor allergic reactions
- QuikClot blood coagulant sponge for localized bleeding
- wound irrigation and disinfectant
- various sizes of sterile gauze pads and wraps
- shears to cut away clothing or bandages
- moleskin for blisters
- petroleum jelly
- triangular bandages with 2 safety pins
- steri-strips for cut closure (make more from duct tape)
- space blanket
- BZK surface and hand disinfectant wipes
- nitrile exam gloves and surgical masks
- wound inspection flashlights
- duct tape (of course) (many emergency uses, even bandages)
- disposable digital thermometers
- small dental type brush
- squeeze bottle of Bactine
- packages of Kleenex
- fingernail clippers

- safety pins
- spare AAA batteries
- cotton swabs
- CPR mask
- insect repellant
- ammonia inhalants
- anti-itch cream
- instant hot and cold packs
- assorted adhesive bandages
- Watergel for burns
- abdominal pads
- bacitracin for first aid
- sharpie marker
- small notebook, with pen
- trauma pack
- Israeli (pressure) bandage
- emergency first aid card
- SAM splint
- eye wash

Stethoscope types

Get a stethoscope because it is necessary to check for patient internal injuries and to monitor patient status. A two-tube stethoscope is much less expensive than a one-tube stethoscope. Many one-tube stethoscopes offered for sale are really two tubes inside of a single tube that binds them together. This overcomes the drawback of two tubes rubbing against each other and causing noise that masks sounds the responder needs to hear.

Purchase a two-tube stethoscope and use strips of duct tape to bind tubes together and reduce noise from rubbing. Leave gaps between duct tape tube-bindings to maintain flexibility. The result is ugly and a clinic would not use it. It works well and is adequate but less costly than purchasing a one-tube stethoscope.

Being able to use a basic stethoscope effectively depends on having training and practice. You can never have enough medical training or practice. The goal is to check a patient for signs of internal injury, like internal bleeding or breathing changes. Be cautious about administering aid when you think what you hear might indicate a problem.

Wound bleeding

Apply direct pressure to a wound while the patient is prone and raise it to a height higher than the heart. Lay the patient flat to put less stress on the heart and blood circulation but make sure that breathing is not compromised. Stabilize the patient and if warranted, immobilize him/her. If you need to immobilize the patient, prevent movement due to cycling between unconsciousness and consciousness.

Displaying first aid emblems on your medical bag focuses supportive attention on you. Display the medical aid symbol, the Red Cross. Display first responder emblems only if you have gone through the necessary certifications. For instance, the paramedic emblem represents training and practical knowledge that is short of going to medical school or nursing school.

Bartering Plan

In an L2 event, bartering will not be a major concern because federal government currency will have value. This changes dramatically in extreme L3 and L4 or L5 events. Valuation reasoning for L3/L4/L5 survival situations is complex and open to interpretation. This is an estimate of what will happen.

In an L3 event (especially social or financial collapse), bartering will replace currency to facilitate buying and selling. Depending on event type and duration, government currency and/or precious metals will regain some or all of their value. In an L4 event, currency and precious metals will never regain full value. In an L5 event, no form of exchange will exist other than bartering.

A bartering plan results from the belief that silver and gold will be useful only in the short term of an L3 event. They will regain value in the long-term. Use paper money as quickly as possible because its value will plummet if the L3 survival event lasts, or is expected to last, a long time. **After acquiring survival supplies,** invest a limited amount of excess funds in precious metals.

Many people own precious metals as a hedge against a crash in stock values and devaluation of currency.

In an L4/L5 survival event currency and precious metals will have limited or no value because people will focus on staying alive (gold has no nutritional value). Use supplies for barter but only if you have more than you need. Food, water, and medical supplies will have the highest value.

Better yet, barter your skills for what you need. Skills will be in high demand because knowing how to fix things so that a repair lasts will be preferred to tinkering until it works again. Skills automatically replenish and it is even better if you have tools to augment your skills. If you need to supply materials, you should ask for a premium valuation for doing the job, before starting.

If an event lasts a long time, currency would be the first form of conventional liquidity to lose value. Silver, gold, and other precious metals and hard goods like antiques, furs, art, and jewelry will lose value too. Items that are commodities today will be in high demand. They are commodities because high quantity mass manufacturing achieves a low price, today.

Food and Cooking Plan

The food and cooking plan uses outdoor grills as long as possible. After that, make wood fires and cook outdoors, even if eating is indoors. Use a small solid fuel stove, and stored solid fuel, only in times when fuel is wet or not available, or when you want to be undetected or don't want visitors. Use your propane primarily for the heater but it is available for cooking.

There are one-burner propane stoves for use in a ventilated area but use a carbon monoxide detector. If weather makes it impossible to cook outdoors, use a propane stove to cook indoors but minimize the amount of long-term cooking. Warming up pre-cooked food is a better option. The reason for using a one-burner stove is to minimize the possibility of carbon monoxide build-up.

Spices improve food taste and disguise the taste of bland or poorly preserved food. If event aftermath extends, available food will get monotonous. Cooking spices often increase cooking odors and make them detectable, giving away your location and that you have supplies. As an alternative, when you want to stay undiscovered, use a 12 VDC stove to heat water, warm up meals and eliminate cooking odors. Use spices sparingly.

One way to achieve a thin or gaunt appearance is to follow a ketogenic diet. Use it to replace fattening foods, not for weight control. In a survival situation, you need to minimize food use. Get accustomed to a ketogenic diet before relying on it.

A ketogenic diet is very similar to the idea of frequent fasting. There are anecdotes that indicate a ketogenic diet has health benefits, when used properly. Once your body is accustomed to a ketogenic diet you can eat foods assuming that excess will be stored as fat and used later.

Dietary requirements for following a ketogenic diet are complex. A ketogenic diet will help you cope with a survival situation but you need to understand how it works. The main point is that your body is good at storing excess consumed food as fat. It later uses the fat when there is not enough food. For this reason, feel free to consume food in quantity when it is available.

The human body can get food energy from processing fat cells (ketosis). Processing fat cells fills the 2200 calories FDA daily consumption recommendation. Your body consumes roughly 2200 calories each day regardless of whether you eat 2200 calories or your body consumes it as fat. Fat has a high energy density. The body becomes accustomed to having fat tissue and wants to consume food to support its existence.

Ketosis is why a person can survive for 30 days without food. Your body is burning fat cells for energy and the typical person has a supply of those. When there are no more fat cells ketosis begins to burn muscle cells, called wasting-away. If this happens, you need to be consuming around 2200 calories of food to be active and to prevent it.

The primary aim of a ketogenic diet is to push the body into ketosis. In ketosis, metabolism shifts from burning carbohydrates to consuming its own fat cells for energy. To achieve ketosis, consume a diet high in healthy fats and very low in sugar and carbohydrates. Without sugar and carbohydrates, the body shifts its focus to making ketones for energy. Ketosis is a process that your body learns; practice it now so it is ready when needed.

As used here, a ketogenic diet is not for weight control and it is not for use during physical effort, e.g., clearing debris. Ketosis will consume muscle if fat is unavailable.

In a survival event, focus on eating protein (meat or beans) and fewer carbohydrates from starchy foods. You may windup storing the protein as fat cells but ketosis will use them.

There are different types of carbohydrates but in general avoid those from starch and get more of them from plants. Things like pasta, rice, and potatoes are starchy foods but eating them is safe, just not often. Book Two of the Plan to Survive series reviews this important but complex subject.

Communications Plan

Communications improve your survival chances. It gives you access to information and enables you to coordinate activity with others. This communications plan uses short-range hand-held radios for coordinating close-in day-to-day activity. They are inexpensive and because they have a limited range, they reduce the chance of giving away your location. They are vitally useful for coordinating security and defense communications.

There are five forms of commonly available radio systems:

UHF General Mobile Radio Service (GMRS)
UHF Family Radio Service (FRS)
UHF Citizens' Band (CB)
VHF Multi-Use Radio Systems (MURS)
VHF marine (as in water) radios

When using a radio, talk in a higher pitch and not as loudly as normal conversation. The person listening to you will understand your message more easily when you use a higher pitch and lesser volume limits feedback.

Very short-range UHF is well suited for most survival tasks. It uses a transmission wave capable of penetrating things like walls and foliage. In a survival situation, you need to coordinate activities (called housekeeping). It limits the ability of others to listen and get an idea of where you are. Longer-range VHF transmissions fit well with longer-range private communication.

UHF transmissions are capable of greater range than VHF transmissions. Due to manufacturing costs, short-range hand-held radios mostly use UHF. UHF signals use a shorter wavelength than VHF signals, for a higher frequency transmission. The higher frequency allows UHF signals to better penetrate objects like glass, walls, and foliage. In a survival event, short-range UHF fulfills most common housekeeping tasks.

Short-range, low-power VHF signals fit the need for coordinating security. Good security means that security coordination needs to stay as local and private as possible. That often means that you don't want those transmissions to range beyond buildings and foliage. You can increase broadcast power and antenna height to increase VHF line-of-sight transmission range.

There is a need to stay informed about law enforcement, fire department, and first responder medical activity. Police and emergency crews are aware that civilians monitor their radio transmissions. Often they have switched to digital broadcasting systems that allow them to encrypt transmissions.

Because you probably do not know first responder transmission encryption keys, digital scanners are not useful. An exception is that receiving digital transmission near mountains is difficult; emergency responders continue to use analog transmissions there.

Mass broadcast media usually tells you a story that authorities sanitize for mass consumption (think "managing" information to support a planned outcome). Monitoring analog and digital transmissions provides additional information to help you read between the lines. Find corroboration before you act.

Some previously encrypted digital transmissions may become unencrypted because encrypting is complex. Encryption equipment breaks or becomes corrupted. Sometimes it is difficult to get codes to field personnel. The bottom line is that an inexpensive analog scanner can be useful but a more expensive analog and digital scanner may be able to give you slightly more of an advantage.

Invest in a scanner antenna to receive weak signals from further away or moving sources. Antennas help scanners monitor line-of-sight UHF and VHF signals. Mount one in your attic to minimize drawing attention to yourself.

Using FRS, MURS, CB, or marine radios does not require a license. Using GMRS radios requires obtaining a license but obtaining it is a formality. Using a CB radio theoretically requires obtaining a license. Unconstrained hobbyist CB use (without a license) and lax enforcement resulted in unclear requirements.

After you have short-range UHF and longer-range VHF radios for daily needs, consider longer distance capability. However, long-range UHF equipment is expensive and you need a license. VHF can have longer-range but not as much as UHF. Longer-range VHF equipment is less expensive than very long-range UHF equipment and licensing to use it is often just a formality.

Handheld VHF MURS and VHF marine radios are more expensive than handheld UHF FRS or GMRS radios. Marine radios often have a low-watt mode for close-by transmission and up to six watts for long-distance transmission. VHF radios have a range from two to 20 miles (with an antenna). A more powerful base station can communicate with low power handheld radios when handheld radios cannot communicate with each other.

Radio systems can be confusing. UHF frequency bands overlap lower frequency VHF bands but you can boost the signal of VHF systems with more power and a higher antenna. The boosts are not as effective with UHF systems. Manufacturing costs are higher for handheld VHF systems. This causes manufacturers to use UHF for mass-market very short-range handheld radios:

- **UHF FRS** (very short range)

    Use FRS radios for L1/L2 and low-level L3 events. FRS radios are widely used and insecure but also inexpensive. Never transmit anything that identifies you, location, supplies status, or defensive posture. They are useful for coordinating tasks. Starting 10/1/19, it is not legal to sell new combined FRS and GMRS radios but you only need one type really.

    Use FRS frequencies to monitor transmissions of others and write down all information. It may seem unimportant now but could be useful later. Use them as little as possible. Use code phrases to convey information with short transmission bursts and obscure intent. It has a realistic range of one-half mile.

- **UHF GMRS** (very short range)

    Use GMRS radios for L1/L2 and low-level L3 events. GMRS radios are common, just not as much as FRS. There are radios that combine FRS radios with GMRS radios in one unit but their sale as a new unit is no longer legal. Consider GMRS frequencies as insecure but use GMRS frequencies for close-in communications.

If you use only the GMRS frequencies of an FRS/GMRS radio, you are avoiding highly used FRS frequencies. Monitor GMRS transmissions of others and write down what you hear. It may seem unimportant now but could be useful later.

It has a range of up to three miles in open terrain but only six blocks in urban terrain. UHF signals penetrate objects, or even foliage, better than VHF signals. This ability works to your advantage because it makes your coordination activities more locally useful. Retail GMRS units often use maximum power, useful for limited range needs but are inexpensive.

- **UHF CB** (short range, but illegally boosting the signal to an intermediate range is possible)

  Using a CB radio theoretically requires obtaining a license. Unconstrained use and lax enforcement resulted in unenforced licensing. Depending on configuration, its range varies from four to seven miles. CB users have congested its frequencies because broadcasting on it is often a hobby.

  A CB radio could be useful for staying in contact with groups. Bypass using CB radio because it is a widely used system susceptible to interference. It is a duplication of the better capabilities of other systems.

  On the other hand, if you have already invested in CB equipment then you can justify using it in addition to FRS/GMRS radios. CB radios would probably be useful in an L4/L5 event because of the reduced population using CB radios..

- **VHF Marine** (short or longer range)

  If your home is inland from a large body of water, use marine radios for L3 and L4/L5 events. It is illegal to use marine radios when one end of the pair is not on or in a body of water but when there is an emergency in an L3/L4/L5 survival situation, expect the rules to be relaxed.

You must stop inland marine radio use when conditions improve and governmental operations resume. However, during an emergency expect a period of governmental tolerance for marine radio use.

If the survival event includes flooding or a tsunami, you are justified using them until the water recedes.

Marine radios have a typical range of up to 10 miles, although it can transmit further when antennas are high enough and more power is used. More power by itself will usually not result in a further transmission distance. Antenna height does improve range because marine VHF radios work on line-of-sight. Buildings and foliage limit line-of-sight transmission.

Inexpensive Cobra handheld marine radios work but are more fragile than Uniden and Standard Horizon models. Cobra radios are advertised as waterproof; they are not, probably not even hard rainproof. Their best use is for stationary lookouts. The lower cost makes them useful for short-range local communication that is more private than FRS or GMRS transmissions. Cobra antennas are built-in and not modifiable.

Use a mix of Cobra, Uniden, and Standard Horizon handheld marine radios for controlling costs and a marine radio base station that can transmit or listen. A base station can relay messages to units that cannot communicate directly.

- **VHF MURS** (short or longer range)

  If your home is near a large body of water, use MURS radios (not marine radios) for transmission privacy reasons. MURS and marine radios are not commonly used. Consider both as insecure though. Marine radios are preferable to MURS radios because manufacturers tend to build marine radios better and their cost is comparable to MURS radios.

  For security reasons, in a survival situation use VHF marine radios if you live inland and MURS equipment if you live near a large body of water. Monitor both marine and MURS transmission frequencies. Baofeng and Dakota Alert MURS equipment are popular. Some Baofeng radios use multiple frequencies; more than just the MURS frequencies. Other radios use VHF frequencies but no MURS frequencies.

- **Very Long-range UHF** (also known as short wave)

  Referred to as Ham radio, using equipment like this for long-distance communication is highly regulated. Knowing the proper and legal use of various types of equipment and federal regulations that govern its use is complicated and a learning experience.

  Luckily, there is the Amateur Radio Relay League (ARRL) to guide obtaining and using licenses. The ARRL represents the interests of Ham radio operators with federal agencies that regulate use of and availability of the frequency spectrum.

  Long distance communication will be invaluable to control general population hysteria and fear. Ham radio information will give people insight to how they will cope with a survival event. Ham radio systems will be one of the only ways to gather information.

Your best bet is to find local Ham radio operators and strengthen your mutual willingness to rely on each other. When the Ham operator realizes that you are trustworthy, you will be able to provide mutual support when a survival event happens. It will be critical to receive information from outside your area and broadcast requests for help (if you broadcast a request for help, you are likely to be one of the first to receive it).

Radio use review

- Never transmit any information that identifies you, location, movements, supplies status, defensive posture, or any operational problems you have.
- Talk in a higher pitch and not as loudly as a normal. The person listening to you will understand your message more easily when you use a higher pitch. The lower volume will limit feedback/squelch.

- Speak slowly and over-pronounce words when you transmit. When transmitting critical information use a phonetic alphabet to spell words.

Military Phonetic Alphabet			
A	Alfa / Alpha	B	Bravo
C	Charlie	D	Delta
E	Echo	F	Foxtrot
G	Golf	H	Hotel
I	India	J	Juliet
K	Kilo	L	Lima
M	Mike	N	November
O	Oscar	P	Papa
Q	Quebec	R	Rome
S	Sierra	T	Tango
U	Uniform	V	Victor
W	Whiskey	X	X-ray
Y	Yankee	Z	Zulu

- Use code phrases to convey information and very short transmission bursts that obscure intent.

- Monitor transmissions and write down what you hear. It may seem unimportant but could be useful later.

- You can extend the range of a radio by using a portable radio as a repeater. Repeaters work by transmitting and receiving on two separate frequencies. To set up a repeater you configure a handheld radio to transmit on the output frequency and enable offset mode for the reception.

- The higher the antenna is, the further you can transmit or receive. Practically, this means that you should use a handheld radio from a higher location but a base station with an antenna tower can relay communications. There are rules about when you can erect an antenna and limits to how high it can be and how much power you can use to broadcast, but enforcement requires an active federal agency.

- There are two scanner types: base station and handheld. A base station can often scan digital and analog frequencies and has some options. A useful option is "close call" that breaks in when it detects close-by transmissions. Scanners can monitor CB, FRS, GMRS, MURS and marine radio signals.

  - Base station scanners use more power than handheld scanners. A base station scanner is nice to have but a handheld analog scanner is more cost effective. Systems often use three-amp and six-amp fuses in DC cigarette lighter plugs, you should have spares. Watch carefully to see if your communication setup uses other fuses because you don't want to be at the mercy of needing a fuse.

  - Handheld scanners are a mobile type that scans a limited number of analog frequencies. They scan civilian VHF only and have few options but find one with the close-call option. Its best use is in the field to detect close transmissions that have implications for field operations. Although there are many choices, the 500 analog channel Uniden BC125AT handheld scanner stands out, mostly for cost and reliability reasons.

  - Have spare fuses for every scanner and radio.

- Digital transmission radios would be private (using encrypted transmissions) but they are very expensive and they are not cost effective or practical.

Addendum

New FCC rules make it possible to misinterpret information contained in this chapter. The Federal Communications Commission (FCC) is changing the rules for selling and using FRS and GMRS radios. The purpose is to increase the number of FRS and GMRS radios that can operate in a given area.

The primary difference between FRS and GMRS under the new regulations is the amount of allowed broadcast power on each channel. The following is the author's summary of new regulations of the FCC, https://www.govinfo.gov/content/pkg/CFR-2017-title47-vol5/xml/CFR-2017-title47-vol5-part95.xml.

FRS radios use narrow-band frequency modulation (NBFM) with a maximum deviation of 2.5-KHz. The channels are spaced at 12.5-KHz intervals. After May 18, 2017, FRS radios sold as new have been limited to a maximum of 2 watts of broadcast power, but enforcement delays to October 1, 2019 are possible. Previously, FRS radios were limited to 0.5-watt for broadcast purposes. FRS radios share channels with GMRS radios.

The FCC does not certify radios for FRS or GMRS service if they exceed limits on power output, have a detachable antenna, allow for unauthorized selection of transmitting frequencies, or can illegally increase power. After December 2017, the FCC no longer accepts applications to certify hand-held FRS or GMRS units providing for transmission in any other radio band.

Handheld FRS radios must use permanently attached antennas. There are tabletop FRS base station radios that use whip antennas. This regulation intentionally limits broadcast and reception, allowing maximum use of available channels in the area of use. FRS manufacturers generally claim exaggerated range. Under normal conditions, with line of sight blocked by a few buildings or trees, FRS has a practical range of about 0.3-1 mile.

- FRS/GMRS Hybrid Radios

  In May 2017, the FCC revised the rules for combined FRS/GMRS radios. Combined radios can only radiate up to 2 watts on 15 of the 22 channels (as opposed to the prior .5 watts). Using over 2 watts, or operation on GMRS repeater input channels, requires licensing.

Effective October 1, 2019, it became unlawful to import, manufacture, or sell radio equipment capable of operating with both GMRS and FRS frequencies

FRS Channels Compared to GMRS			
Channel	Frequency MHz	FRS ERP* Restriction	GMRS ERP Restriction
1	462.5625	Up to 2 watts	Up to 5 watts
2	462.5875	Up to 2 watts	Up to 5 watts
3	462.6125	Up to 2 watts	Up to 5 watts
4	462.6375	Up to 2 watts	Up to 5 watts
5	462.6625	Up to 2 watts	Up to 5 watts
6	462.6875	Up to 2 watts	Up to 5 watts
7	462.7125	Up to 2 watts	Up to 5 watts
8	467.5625	Up to 0.5 watts	Up to 0.5 watt
9	467.5875	Up to 0.5 watts	Up to 0.5 watts
10	467.6125	Up to 0.5 watts	Up to 0.5 watts
11	467.6375	Up to 0.5 watts	Up to 0.5 watts
12	467.6625	Up to 0.5 watts	Up to 0.5 watts
13	467.6875	Up to 0.5 watts	Up to 0.5 watts
14	467.7125	Up to 0.5 watts	Up to 0.5 watts
15	462.5500	Up to 2 watts	Up to 50 watts
16	462.5750	Up to 2 watts	Up to 50 watts
17	462.6000	Up to 2 watts	Up to 50 watts
18	462.6250	Up to 2 watts	Up to 50 watts
19	462.6500	Up to 2 watts	Up to 50 watts
20	462.6750	Up to 2 watts	Up to 50 watts
21	462.7000	Up to 2 watts	Up to 50 watts
22	462.7250	Up to 2 watts	Up to 50 watts

* ERP (Effective Radiated Power)

- GMRS has eight channels for repeater input
- No FRS unit shall exceed 0.5 watt ERP on channels 8-14. FRS Channels 15-22 are shared with GMRS but must be under 2 watts ERP. However, if the device includes any of the following channels (467.5500, 467.5750, 467.6000, 467.6250, 467.6500, 467.6750, 467.7000, and 467.7250 MHz) a GMRS license is required. Benefits of a GMRS license include the ability to use repeaters, run higher power (up to 50 watts), and utilize external antennas.

The bottom line is that the FCC is increasing the number of possible FRS and GMRS active radios in a specific area by decreasing the allowable power of each FRS radio. This allows a greater number of FRS radios to be used in a specific area because if they are distributed evenly around the area the range of each is less likely to interfere with use of another. No FRS license will be required.

You can increase the transmission range of GMRS radios because they can have greater power and a better antenna. A 10-year license to use GMRS radios will cost $70 on October 1, 2019. Enforcement is uncertain.

Use FRS or GMRS radios close to your bug-in for coordination purposes. Use them in the low-power mode because you do not want to deal with eavesdropping.

Survival Rules

Before ending this chapter, please review the following rules of survival conduct. They address how you might want to react in a survival situation. Realize that these rules apply differently depending on the type of the survival event.

In an L1/L2 event, do not use or apply these rules. In a less intense L3 event, use judgment to apply the rules. Pay attention to the availability and reliability of law enforcement. Apply the rules fully in more intense L3 or L4/L5 events.

Copy the rules onto single sheet of paper (front and back), so that only the rules will be on the page. The rules are on a single page in the paperback version of this book. Laminate the sheet of rules. Each of your survival group members should have a copy.

This page intentionally blank.

Survival Rules

Do not apply these rules to L1/L2 events and use discretion in an L3 event. Use them in L4/L5 events.

Rule 1 – Maintain a low profile. You want to be invisible and quiet, especially at night. Wear a hooded sweatshirt to cover your cleanliness (which will stand out as "not normal") and use a non-descript backpack. Use night vision equipment at night, so you can see nighttime movements, because people think the cover of darkness hides activity. Take advantage of this.

Rule 2 – Do not shoot anyone, if possible (but don't hesitate when necessary). Once you fire a weapon, you attract attention and you will be in danger. The family of whomever you shoot may seek revenge if forced to shoot someone. They won't care about your reason.

Desperate intruders will force you to stop them. Make no compromise that jeopardizes your survival group. Shooting is a last resort. Keep in mind that bad people don't have rules.

Trust no one! A situation often demands shoot or be shot. When a situation warrants be first to go violent. End any confrontation decisively. Leave no doubt.

Rule 3 – Prevent injury to anyone in your group. Once you or a group member is injured, recovery is not certain. Treat every skin break as a potential infection. Warn the patient about the need to report signs of infection. You must have a trauma kit readily available to stop bleeding.

Rule 4 – Keep moving because a moving target is hard to engage. Use the tactic of firing a firearm and immediately moving because firearm blast gives away position. Staying in motion applies to knife attacks too. Arrange objects so there is only one way to get in, and make it narrow to limit movement.

Rule 5 – Defending your survival group from inside your bug-in traps you inside. Inside you have no idea what is going on outside. Outside you know what is happening. With night vision equipment, you see what is going on at night. Consider protecting your home from the outside during the first three weeks or so.

Rule 6 – Befriend your neighbors ahead of time. They can be part of your defense team, or your foe. A team of neighbors is a great defense against looters. Choose friends wisely.

Rule 7 – Scam-proof your brain. When people are desperate, truth goes out the door. People will approach you with stories of need. **Do not let anyone in your perimeter, no one!** Have compassion but send them on their way. You are your own fire department, police department, and hospital so beware of seemingly harmless offers of help.

Rule 8 – Death-proof your brain. Many people are going to die. Unprepared people are going to run out of water, food, and medicine. Looters will overrun or kill some people. Death will be all around you, be prepared. If you give away your supplies, you will die too. Everyone heard the warnings but some chose not to respond. It is their responsibility to protect their families.

Rule 9 – It will get better. No matter how bad the storm the sun always comes out. How long that will be no one knows; it could be days, weeks, months, or years. You stuck it out. You are not a quitter. Fear will not overtake you. Other "I Can and I Will" people will survive.

Notes: Who Will Survive

Notes: Who Will Survive

Chapter 4
When It Happens

This chapter addresses situations you can expect and their importance to survival planning. Consult multiple sources and consider the probability of one event triggering another event. Consider the probabilities of other events, e.g., a global famine initiated by widespread severe weather, forcing governments to steal from their neighbors, starting a war.

As a possibility, North Korea suffers a wide famine due to severe weather effects. Embargoes make the famine worse, forcing the regime to consider using nuclear weapons as their only advantage. They attack South Korea to get food and that draws in the United States, who is committed to protecting their ally.

You enhance your foresight by increasing the number of sources of information you use. If after considering the information your intuition is that an event is going to happen you can decide on an immediate bug-in. This means that you bug-in at home and prepare for an intensifying event. Call-in sick, but do not abandon your livelihood until you are certain of the event.

Short-term vs. Long-term Events

Consider whether the survival event is L1/L2 (probably regional and short-term), L3 (probably regional/national and long-term), or L4/L5 (probably global and very long-term).

Be sure to include duration of event aftermath in your estimation of the event. If you believe the event is short-term, then you also believe that external aid will arrive, so definitely bug-in. If you believe it is long-term then external aid will be sporadic, if at all. If you believe it is long-term, you should bug-in but consider bugging-out. If you believe the event is very long-term and that there will be no meaningful external aid, bug-out.

Bugging-in means you are in your home (possibly camping in the backyard). You can access and use preparations you have made. You need to make do with what you have, or as the military says, "improvise and adapt." Priority survival needs will be, water, food, shelter, and security. Augment water and food with what you find foraging and scavenging.

A big difference is that for short-term events, stores will open and you can restock supplies that you used. For long-term events, there may only be sporadic restocking, if at all. You may want to restock food and medical supplies but it will not be possible. Don't count on resupplying your dwindling supplies. For a long-term event, storing a year of supplies may not be enough.

A basic concept is that if you are prepared others will want your survival supplies. The more intense the survival event the more desperate other survivors will become. Desperation breeds using violence to get what you want. A possible non-violent option is to have sacrificial supplies that you can give away. However, that implies you have more.

Getting to Your Bug-in

No matter which event occurs, there is a good chance you will not be at home when it happens. Most L1 and L2 events occur with some advance warning because they tend to be extreme weather oriented. Some L1 and L2 events have no advance warning. In order to bug-in you first must survive the chaos of the initial event and get back to your home and your supplies.

Two types of preparations help you get home, an Every Day Carry (EDC) kit and a Get Home Bag (GHB). Use them as titled. Keep the EDC with you when you are within about 30 miles of your home and the GHB if local, but more than 30 miles from home. Keep them minimal, assuming most of your supplies are pre-positioned at your bug-in. In no case should you attempt to take your EDC kit or GHB into any facility prohibiting any of the items.

If you are traveling, the further away from home you are the more you should have your Bug-Out Bag (BOB) with you. If you are flying, check the BOB as luggage or bring it as carry-on luggage, with necessary air safety modifications. Reserve using supplies in a Bug-Out Pack (BOP) for when you leave a bug-in.

- **EDC**

  An EDC kit consists of items you use to get to your GHB but it can help you get home. An EDC kit is minimal and depends on your location. You may need to accommodate those around you to prevent a confrontation. Keep your EDC kit items in a non-descript waist pack or small sling pack that you can easily carry unobtrusively. It will receive intense wear and tear so get one that is sturdy and well built.

- **GHB**

  A GHB is larger than an EDC because it contains supplies to sustain you while returning home. Being larger, the natural place would be in a car but if your workplace or traveling allows, keep it with you. Use a non-descript small backpack or full-size sling pack to carry your GHB. It will receive intense wear and tear so get one that is sturdy and well built.

Essential Supplies for L1-L5 Events

Assemble the minimum group of supplies. These supplies are necessary for all L1-L5 events. They should be supplemented for specific types of events:

1 knives for self-defense, utility use, food prep
2 weather alert radio with battery backup
3 stored food and water
4 portable shelter
5 portable first-aid bag, with extra basic supplies
6 filtering water pitcher, with extra filters
7 plastic trash bags
8 flashlights and a lantern, with extra batteries
9 EDC and GHB, to get to a bug-in location
10 BOB and BOP (if forced to evacuate your bug-in)

A low cost (but cost effective and reliable) alternative to item two is the Uniden BC355N 800 MHz 300-Channel Base/Mobile Scanner radio, it is both an analog broadcast scanner and weather alert radio. This base station scanner has features handhelds do not have. It does not monitor digital transmissions.

Stored food and water (items three and four) maintain your ability to respond to situations in the aftermath of an event. Realize that wet food has dissolved oxygen in the liquid. Dissolved oxygen causes food to oxidize and spoil. Oils go rancid in stored food. Dry food in sealed packaging is the best option. There is a further review of storage foods in Book Two of the *Plan to Survive* series.

Chapter 3 of this book reviews the contents of a medical bag (item five). The bag must be portable so one person can use it to respond to a need for medical attention which is likely away from where it is. Moving someone who is injured may make the injury worse. Book Two of this *Plan to Survive* series examines its contents in detail.

A filtering water pitcher (item six) is necessary because in most events access to drinkable water is limited. Other sources of water may be available but you need to be able to purify them. Play it safe and filter/purify any questionable water. Beware of water source; no filter removes all dissolved chemicals.

You will need plastic bags (item seven) to store trash, so trash does not attract vermin or become a health hazard. In addition to this basic function, you will find many other uses for them, e.g., temporary shelters, emergency raincoats, carrying loose gear, organizing food, etc., but store the thicker variety (3 mils thick). Keep them away from vermin and marauding animals.

The need for flashlights and a lantern (item eight) is critical because electricity will be unreliable. It will probably be unavailable for days or weeks. Orient to daylight hours. Storing spare batteries is crucial; see the discussion in Chapter 3.

When to Bug-in and When to Bug-out

Bugging-in means sheltering-in-place. Most people cannot afford to make elaborate bug-in plans. Make your home your shelter. Listen to your emergency weather radio for what to expect and updates on conditions. Watch how the people around you react and what they do. Realize authorities will sanitize information to minimize hysteria and prevent general population panic.

Realize that if you choose to bug-out later, it is impossible to take all your supplies. Consider the example of water. It may seem a critical supply to take if you bug-out but it is heavy and bulky. Take a water filter instead. Be prepared to leave supplies behind. Stay at home as long as reasonable, before you abandon supplies.

Although your home is your shelter, you can enhance it as by planning to use it to bug-in. You may decide on a conditional bug-in, which means that you stay at home and prepare for an intensifying event. Call-in sick but don't abandon your job and livelihood until you are certain of the survival event.

Bugging-in means you are in your home, or possibly camping in your backyard or near your home. It also means that you have access to stored supplies and preparations you have made. Make do with what you have: improvise and adapt. Foraging augments water and food.

What to Expect from an L2 Event

Many sources predict severe weather (L2 events). With enough lead-time, you can prepare. The problem is that this is a widely communicated warning that comes out when there is event certainty. Warnings are often geographically imprecise and you will not have enough time to gather supplies once it is more specific. On top of that, expect panic buying strips stores of all supplies, as soon as a warning comes out.

Think of what a panicking public can do to a grocery store. A supermarket typically has only a 3-day supply of food and commodities. Your best bet is to have supplies of food and water stored and pick-up supplies that most people will not think of at first. Pick up supplies like first aid items, e.g., bandages, antibiotic cream, splints, pain relievers, fever reducers, antihistamines, etc., and later trade them for what you need.

Go to big-box hardware stores, local pharmacies, and smaller grocery stores. These are your best source for supplies, while a panicked public focuses on supermarkets. Bring cash because credit cards may not work.

Coping after an L2 event

L2 events like severe weather will make travel difficult. Because these events are temporary, you need to be able to wait for them to end. Saying that L2 events are temporary is only partially true. Consider survival situations that people face after a hurricane, tornado, or earthquake. Although the actual event is short lived, you must still deal with the aftermath.

Depending on what type of assistance you expect to receive, you need to decide what you can rely on. Assistance may be sporadic and those providing it may use acceptance to control you, i.e., where you go, what you do, when you do it, and how you do it. Think of the problems with temporary shelters, like the New Orleans Superdome after hurricane Katrina.

A general recommendation is to maintain independence from this type of control as long as possible. Have your own supplies to rely on and supplement them with emergency assistance supplies, without placing you or your survival group under the control of others.

Don't hesitate to accept medical aid. It is easy to wait too long and have a minor need become life threatening, especially since disease and infection will be common.

Example 1: 2005 Hurricane Katrina in New Orleans

Do you remember how New Orleans tried to cope with Hurricane Katrina by using a temporary shelter at the New Orleans Superdome? This response to a regional L2 event had worsening consequences because of poor preparation and mismanagement.

Cascading effects caused substantial changes that made life for survivors not just difficult but life threatening.

Even when you thought you were safe in a hospital, the aftermath caused problems. It did not help that police were unreliable (leading to calling in the National Guard).

Example 2: 2012 Super Storm Sandy

Another L2 event to consider is the failure of managing Super Storm Sandy in 2012. Event planning, response to the ongoing event, and dealing with the aftermath were inadequate. Storm surge caused most of the deaths. Electrical power outages affected more than eight million people, with some outages lasting for weeks. Gasoline rationing lasted over two weeks.

All this happened even though there was a massive influx of assistance. Infrastructure damage delayed its effective distribution and use. High population density in the affected area not only increased immediate aftermath effects but hampered ongoing relief effort. Too often individuals attempted to take advantage of the event to improve their lives and finances. Years later, some of the housing and infrastructure is still unusable.

Example 3: 2010 Haiti Earthquake

An example of waiting too long for medical attention is Haiti. An earthquake at first caused limited disease. Survivors contracted diseases that were made worse by not following isolation and quarantine methods soon enough. The result was that they wound up spreading communicable diseases among themselves and overwhelming limited medical aid.

Supplementing L2 supplies

In all three of these L2 examples, the aftermath had a greater impact than expected. The general population was complacent with the status quo of daily living. They waited too long to try to acquire the supplies they needed.

As a result, they experienced high prices, shortages, waiting lines and even physical competition to get remaining supplies. Additional L2 supplies to supplement basic L1 supplies include:

more stored water
more stored food
small tent(s)
BOB (the contents are not for immediate use)
generator (perhaps share this expense with a neighbor)
small batteries
glass break alarms (for windows in your bug-in)
another battery powered lantern
exterior and interior emergency motion lighting

Book Two of the *Plan to Survive* series goes into detail discussing the merits of these items.

What to Expect from an L3 Event

In an L3 event, assistance will be limited in timeliness, quantity, and quality. L3 events usually have long-term and far-reaching consequences that affect you. For example, in Puerto Rico not only did the electrical grid fail but also users started loading it as repairs progressed, causing new failures, and blackouts.

You can expect high priority needs, like police, to receive available assistance first. Other services needed to maintain order could be military troops to control rioting and looting, fire trucks and personnel to fight infrastructure fires, and medical facilities. With all the diverted assistance, you will often be on your own to protect and preserve your survival group and your home.

Looters are probably the worst L3 event scenario because they appear suddenly and have little sympathy for your plight. Sometimes they are just trying to survive but often they just want to sell your supplies to other survivors. Right now, the most dangerous job in Venezuela might be driving a truck. Looters are stopping and hijacking trucks at gunpoint to get supplies before distribution centers.

Coping after an L3 event

Surviving an L3 event is not complex. Just be aware that the situation can change and that you must stay informed. Compare information sources so you can catch irregularities. Overseas news broadcasts are a good source.

Even though New Orleans prepared for Hurricane Katrina, there were worsening consequences. Although the event itself was an extreme L2 event, it has implications for an L3 event. Especially concerning is that aftermath changes could be so gradual that you are lulled into complacency.

If a rapid change develops you might not recognize it soon enough. The worst situation is not realizing that a solution may lead to other dangers. As an example, Puerto Ricans drank water from contaminated sources because they could not get clean drinking water, then they got sick.

Because L3 events are usually regional, you can expect assistance from geographically distant sources not directly affected. This can change rapidly if the disaster spreads or cannot be contained. You may find yourself having to be self-sufficient and depending on your own supplies (and bartering with them) for what you need. Make decisions assuming there will be no external aid.

Given the possible redeployment of assistance resources to higher priority needs, you should limit your dependence on external aid. Do this so you can revert to total self-sufficiency when you need to. Depending on external aid might work at first but if it interrupts your dependence works against you.

Example 1: 1980 Mount St. Helens Eruption

The 1980 Mount St. Helens eruption is the only recent L3 event in the U.S. mainland. The eruption occurred in a less densely populated area. Damage from the eruption was mostly contained. Area damage was mostly wilderness destruction but the ash cloud affected air travel. Most of the dead resulted from the pyroclastic flow (a fluidized mass of rock fragments, gases, mud, and ash). Stay out of flow channels when there is seismic activity.

Example 2: 2016 New Zealand Earthquake

Think about the mostly good example of L3 event management that occurred dealing with the short and long-term effects of the 2016 earthquake and tsunami that hit Wellington and Christ Church, New Zealand. The Wellington Regional Emergency Management Office (WREMO) responded but did not have adequate stockpiled supplies.

Luckily, the earthquake was a regional event and external assistance arrived quickly. If this L3 disaster had been more widely spread there would have been great difficulty getting external assistance to all those affected.

Example 3: 2011 Tōhoku Earthquake and Tsunami

Another positive example of how L3 event management dealt with the short- and long-term effects is the 2011 Tōhoku earthquake and tsunami. The epicenter of the earthquake was off the coast. The ensuing tsunami killed many people and caused massive damage. The earthquake itself did not cause extensive damage but the force of the tsunami did.

The Tōhoku earthquake damaged five nuclear reactors at two nuclear power plants and caused reactor shutdowns at three more sites. Radiation release caused mass hysteria but this event points out how event aftermath consequences cause indirect effects. Radiation leakage has continued, years after the event.

Earthquakes and tsunamis in the Middle East, Indonesia, and the Western part of South America, hurricanes in Central America and North America, and typhoons and volcanic activity in the Far East seem to be getting more frequent and intense. **Many people in these areas are subsisting on minimum income and cannot afford to prepare – you can**.

Supplementing L3 supplies

A good takeaway from these examples is that your location might render your supplies useless or infrastructure damage makes access to them difficult. For example, a pushcart can relocate critical supplies when an event compromises their initial location. You could also use pull-along sleds and snowshoes on snow and ice where it is difficult to use a cart, but for the same purpose.

Starting with L3 events, stored supplies get complex. An L3 event will be intense and the aftermath will last a long time. Additional L3 supplies to supplement L2 supplies include:

- more stored food
- more stored water
- water filtration systems
- laundry bleach for water disinfection (time limited)
- calcium hypochlorite (for long-term water disinfection)
- coconut oil (for cooking)
- iodized salt
- cooking utensils
- method for heating food
- cast iron pots and pans

- eating accessories (e.g., cups and plates)
- sturdy clothing
- OTC pills
- OTC salves and ointments
- OTC wound irrigation and coagulants
- Other OTC medical items
- pandemic supplies
- antibiotics
- bathroom tissue
- chemical toilet
- bucket porta-potty(s)
- laundry supplies
- cleaning supplies
- cold weather sleeping bags (maintain accessibility)
- sleeping systems
- blankets
- fire extinguishers
- "Biohazard – Do Not Enter" warning tape
- smoke detectors (ionization detection)
- carbon monoxide (CO) detectors
- video cameras (outside and inside)
- plastic film for windows
- pre-cut plywood for windows, use 3" coarse thread screws
- secure doors
- black tempera powder (to blackout windows)
- open window alarms
- broken window alarms
- more flashlights and lanterns
- outdoor lights
- Kevlar tunics
- Kevlar arm sleeves
- knives and hatchets
- machete
- knife sharpeners

- sharpening systems
- sharpening stones
- low cost rifle scope or binoculars, for distance viewing
- printed books
- DC and AC devices and distribution
- gasoline transfer system
- propane heater
- 12V DC lantern
- signaling devices (mirror, smoke bomb, flare, etc.)
- base station scanner (analog and digital)
- handheld scanner (analog)
- base station VHF marine radio*
- MURS scanner*
- FRS, GMRS, and marine radios*
- all-purpose radio AM/FM/MW/SW
- weather alert battery-solar-hand crank radio
- gas and water shut-off tools
- rope, at least 50 feet
- adult tricycle
- buckets (2 ½ and 5-gallon buckets, some food-grade)
- BOP

* Reverse MURS and marine radios if your bug-in is near water.

What to Expect from an L4 Event

An L4 event is national or global in scope, with high probability that air and sea travel will spread any related pandemic effects. It is easy to speculate about L4 events, such as:

- asteroid impact
- pandemic
- nuclear war
- dramatic climate shift effects

- ice age
- EMP
- wide area CME (different from an EMP)
- social collapse
- insect extinction
- super-volcano eruption

Fortunately, the probability of an L4 event is remote. Life would be traumatic while we recover but recovery is possible and probable. There will probably be no assistance, or if there is be wary of conditions. Remember what politicians tend to think in terms of, "Never let a good crisis go to waste."

Coping after an L4 event

Surviving an L4 event is complex because there are several massive event scenarios and adequately preparing for each implies extensive stockpiling. The best you can reasonably expect to do is to add to your L3 event supplies in order to build a general-purpose stockpile and plan to repurpose supplies and scavenge or barter for what you need.

Supplementing L4 supplies

Following are suggestions for L4 event supplies supplementation. The range of possible events and their severity makes it difficult to itemize a comprehensive list. Depending on the event, a lot of this list will not be applicable, so see this as suggestions only:

- more stored food
- more stored water
- iodine beads (to disinfect water)
- butter
- non-iodized salt
- white vinegar

- paper towels
- paper plates and napkins; plastic cups and eating utensils
- food extras (like condiments and spices)
- large tent with accessories
- cold and wet weather clothing
- dental kit
- emergency first-aid/surgery kit
- more medical supplies
- personal hygiene supplies
- carpet sweeper
- mop
- broom and dust pan
- hunting and fishing equipment
- e-books (to simplify tasks)
- photovoltaic (PV) system
- large batteries (for PV system, deep-cycle)
- candles
- propane stoves (with battery powered CO detectors)
- propane burner (single burner, portable)
- oil supplies
- stored energy (propane, gasoline, diesel, firewood…)
- electric (AC and DC) fans
- portable water heater
- hand tools
- repairs and woodworking tools
- tool carrying bag
- repair and sewing materials
- large and small tarps
- garden cart
- wheelbarrow
- gasoline and electric chainsaws
- spare chains for chainsaws
- ad hoc EMP shielding (heavy duty aluminum foil, etc.)
- motion detection systems

- PV electrical system and supplies
- small batteries
- more flashlights and lanterns
- heavy duty soldering kit
- night vision (NV) monocular(s)
- forward looking infra-red monocular (FLIR, thermal)
- infrared flashlight
- battery charging system reserved for NV devices
- small aluminum trashcan, for desk area EMP protection
- heirloom seeds
- camp knife

Book Two of the *Plan to Survive* series details the merits and uses of these items.

What to Expect from an L5 Event

There has never been an L5 event in the history of humanity. An L5 event could take the form of a space borne fatal pathogen, major super-volcano eruption, ice age, global CME, black hole, gamma ray burst, etc. There is little chance of surviving L5 events but if you do, life will be unimaginable. Trying to predict what survival supplies you might need is a hopeless exercise.

Humanity has existed for a small length of time, compared to how long the planet has existed. There is plenty of time for an L5 event to happen, eventually.

The most massive L5 event in the history of this planet may have been a super volcanic eruption in Siberia 250 million years ago. It spewed out so much magma that the magma eventually covered an area greater than that of the continental United States. What is mystifying is that the eruption occurred in an area, Siberia, not known for volcanic activity.

There was so much carbon dioxide and methane released that the global level rose to three times normal. The increased level killed animal life on land and in oceans and the temperature of the world rose at least 20° F.

It might be that the impact of a large asteroid impact killed off the dinosaurs, other animals, plant life, and most ocean life was an L5 event. It is likely that a large asteroid hitting the Earth will happen again. Stephen Hawking, the late brilliant British cosmologist, said that humans must colonize other planets to ensure species continuation. Talk about planning to survive!

The consensus of preppers and survivalists suggests that to survive an L4/L5 event you need a two-year supply of food and water to sustain each person in your survival group until you can grow crops again. Even if you succeed in making it to the point of creating a sustainable life you can expect your life to be difficult and one of ceaseless manual labor with extreme loneliness and boredom. There would be periods of panic, depression, and desperation.

Survivalists lead a life of preparation for an L4/L5 event and are mutually supportive. They lead lives to the point of saying and doing things that are very different from how everyone else pursues life. They could be right in their assessment of the need but realize that L5 events have a very low probability of ever happening.

Notes: When It Happens

Notes: When It Happens

Chapter 5
Where an Event Might Happen

The top line summary is that there is a difference between what this chapter focuses on and what you can expect to happen where you live. Preparing for survival events where you live may mean that you should selectively choose from all preparations listed here. Basic preparations (see Chapter 9) are common to all events. Given the relative probabilities of events, you need to choose the lifestyle that you can and want to live with.

An L1 event has limited impact on your lifestyle. Things change when you start considering the probability and aftermath of L2 events. L2 events include severe weather, minor rioting, flooding, ice storm, high winds, tornadoes, hurricanes, tidal flooding, snowstorm, heat wave, drought… Parts of the United States are more susceptible to L2 and even L3 events than other parts of the country:

East Coast states have hurricanes, floods, and blizzards.
West Coast states have storms, forest fires, and earthquakes.
Midwest and South states have flooding and tornadoes.
Plains states have violent storms, flooding, and tornadoes.
Rocky Mountain states have blizzards and forest fires.
Northern states have blizzards and flooding.
Southern states have heat waves and very high humidity.
Northwest states have forest fires
Southwest states have heat waves and forest fires.*

*Heat waves are not as severe in the mountains. There is less risk of forest fire due to a lower population.

There are geologic events so intense that their higher probability in the west warrants emphasis. Occurrence of a Cascadian subduction zone rupture or earthquake along the San Andreas Fault would cause massive destruction and loss of life. If either ruptured there would be wide-ranging and long-term consequences not only for the U.S. but for the entire world.

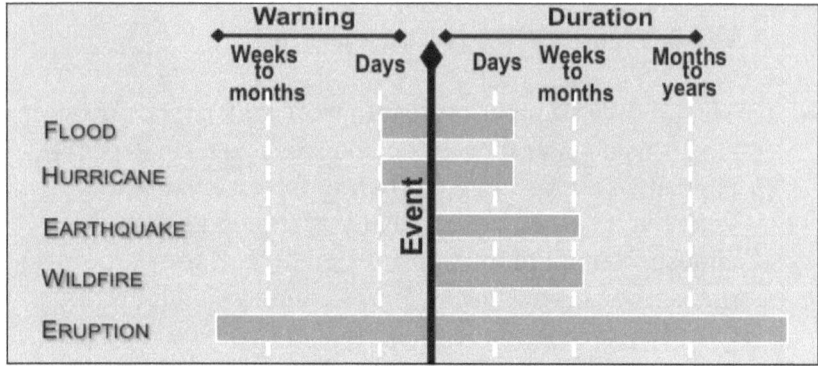

Figure 5. US Geological Survey, Department of the Interior/USGS

No matter where you live, some form of extreme weather or seismic event is possible. There are parts of the U.S. that are less prone to such events. It needs to be pointed out that the greater the level of infrastructure the greater the probability of external assistance. Two relatively safe areas in the U.S. are Nevada/Arizona/New Mexico and North Dakota/Montana/Idaho/Wyoming.

Nevada/Arizona/New Mexico

Nevada, Arizona, and New Mexico are prone to their own types of extreme weather. However, these three states experience less frequent weather events. Living in the mountains may remove you from deadly heat waves and major flooding (just do not live by rivers or creeks), but prepare for forest fires and blizzards. Intense forest fire heat can cause spontaneous combustion.

The potential for forest fire damage declines by carefully choosing where you establish your home and by clearing away fire fuel near your home. Even grass can sustain a fire long enough for it to ignite a wood frame house.

You can deal with blizzards if you have stored supplies. Dust masks are useful in a blizzard because they trap warm moist air. Use the masks so you can go outside when there is ash in the air.

An unfortunate reality is that Nevada, Arizona, and New Mexico are on roads for evacuating Los Angeles and California. If there are L3 or L4 events that affect the Los Angeles area (or Dallas-Fort Worth or El Paso) you can expect a flood of survivors from those areas to move through looking for supplies.

Locate in the mountains and away from the major travel arteries of I10 and I40. Mountains have their own unique events to deal with and a sparse population that can help you (join local groups so locals know you). You have a better chance controlling event effects there, more than you do controlling a refugee exodus.

North Dakota/Montana/Idaho/Wyoming

The North Dakota/Montana area sits on rock that is the southern portion of the Laurentian Plateau. Most of Canada rests on these igneous (once molten) rocks but the plateau extends into North Dakota/Montana. The bedrock is so solid that it limits seismic activity. Because the area is sparsely populated, there would be little intrusion by L3 or L4 event survivors.

The bad news, other than the bitterly cold winters, is that the area is home to much of the U.S. nuclear weapon arsenal. This makes radiation leakage a probable complication in the aftermath of an L3 or L4 event. Considering the jet stream effect (wind blowing mostly west to east or sometimes WNW to ESE), risking your survival downwind of this area is a possible problem.

Survivalists often include western Oregon and western Washington with this area. They refer to the six-state area as the American Redoubt. They promote the area as having enough space to accommodate people moving there. The area often experiences forest fires and blizzards but due to the jet stream, western Oregon/Washington will experience little of the effects of radiation leakage from nuclear weapons.

Extreme Seismic Events

There are extreme seismic events that are potentially devastating. They are so extreme that their occurrence would affect areas far from immediately adjacent areas. The potential for rupture of the Cascadian subduction zone or along the San Andreas fault would cause massive destruction. Eruption(s) at Yellowstone would also.

If either the Cascadian subduction zone or San Andreas fault ruptured; or the Cascade Mountains, or the Rocky Mountains became seismically active, expect long-term and wide-ranging effects. Although dormant now, they could become active again, as Mount Saint Helens did. It was supposedly dormant.

The Cascadian subduction zone has the potential for catastrophic damage. Seismic damage from a Cascadian under seas fault rupture will be minimal but the tsunami is another matter. Destruction of infrastructure and deaths would be massive.

After a Cascadian subduction zone rupture, the next most likely extreme seismic event is a super-volcano. Depending on event scale, it could have similar vast effect on national and global economies. Super-volcano particulates suspended in the atmosphere would cause massive crop failures by changing the climate and blocking light.

A large tsunami would have vast global economic impact, no matter where it physically hit. Figure 6 may give you an idea of the damage that could happen from a tsunami, most likely caused by a seismic event in the ocean.

Figure 6. Tsunami caused by an ocean seismic event

The largest super-volcano in the world is Yellowstone National Park in the United States. It has a subterranean magma chamber four times larger than the world's next largest super-volcano (also in the U.S.) Seismic activity of either would cause L3 or L4 events but remember the greater the destruction the lower the probability. This is a list of the world's largest known super-volcanoes:

Yellowstone caldera (northwestern Wyoming, U.S.)
Long Valley caldera (east-central California, U.S.)
Lake Toba (North Sumatra, Indonesia)
Taupo caldera (New Zealand)
Campi Flegrei (southern west coast, Italy)
Valles caldera (central northern New Mexico, U.S.)
Aira caldera (southern Japan)

Although the probability of a super-volcano eruption is very low, it will happen. There is almost no chance that any eruption will stop at a low level. An eruption relieves magma pressure. Magma pressure built up because there was no ability to release it. Once there is then the eruption will continue until magma pressure is completely relieved.

Infrastructure Damage

Expect infrastructure damage starting with L3 events. It will limit the ability of people to travel and for disaster relief to arrive. Since disease is often communicable, the spread of disease will slow. Don't expect immediate external assistance of any type (water, food, fuel or medical) when there is infrastructure damage. Be prepared to survive on stored supplies and don't take actions based on assuming that external relief will arrive.

Use foraging, scavenging, and bartering to extend your length of survival. However, realize that leaving your home to forage, scavenge, or barter exposes you. If seen you could compromise your safety, group safety, your supplies, or your location.

Extreme weather events often damage roads and bridges in a way that makes repairs take a long time. The most common damage is from flooding. Rushing water damages a wide area and the ground that a structure is built-on. Beware of foundation damage.

Seismic events often create simpler to repair damage. Seismic damage may shift the ground under a structure and damage it. Flooding usually only damages the ground. Use a temporary structure to replace it quickly if repairs are too time consuming.

Because flooding is more common, expect increasing flood related effects. This may mean limited availability of food and fuel. If you live in a rural location, it could also mean long-term isolation. A group of isolated people may over-react and attempt to ensure their own safety. If you are in this type of situation, the need to store long-term survival supplies should be an even higher priority.

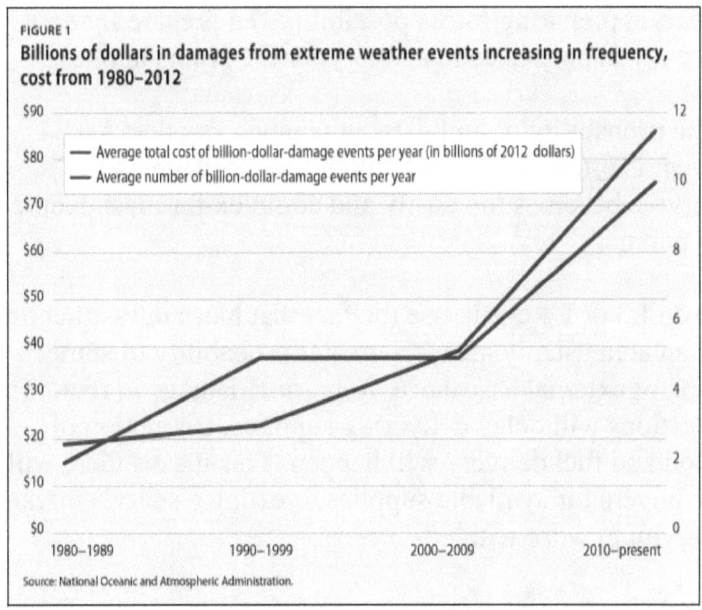

Figure 7. Extreme weather building and infrastructure damage

Preparing to Cope with Infrastructure Damage

For an L3 event, shelter-in-place for as long as possible without leaving your home and let mass hysteria and an urge to bug-out burn itself out. An interpretation of the graph in Figure 7 indicates that infrastructure repair is getting more frequent, complex, costly, and time consuming. Don't use up your supplies too fast, expecting assistance that may not come soon enough.

Infrastructure damage will limit your ability to resupply. Don't choose a bug-in or bug-out location that makes you dependent on timely deliveries. In just an L2 event, cleaning out supermarkets in a matter of hours and gas station lines are common in all events. You avoid delivery disruption problems by relocating to less stressed areas that have reasonably good infrastructure.

The probability of an L3 event is significant enough to warrant preparing for its possibility. To prepare for an L3 event you only need to add to your L2 event supplies.

The probability of an L4 event is much smaller. An L4 event is often the point at which further planning to survive becomes too costly and complex for most people to pursue.

In an L3 or L4 event, use the fact that more infrastructure in an area usually means a greater probability of some type of external assistance. Repairing damage in remote locations will delay delivering supplies. Disruption of food and fuel delivery will happen. This means there will be buyers for available supplies, creating a seller's market for you to work with.

Consider the cost effectiveness of trying to prepare for an L4 or L5 event. Events like these have a low probability of occurring. Supplies to prepare for these events are extensive and you need extensive knowledge and training to use them effectively. Surviving in an L4 or L5 environment will be more likely because of knowledge and skills. Invest your financial resources in acquiring knowledge and skills, after you stock basic supplies.

The Survivalist Point of View

Survivalists spend most of their lives preparing to survive an L4 or even L5 event, sharing thoughts on survival and finding ways to stretch resources. In an L4 event, infrastructure damage is more extensive than in an L3 event. In an L5 event, any still existing infrastructure would be too unreliable or too dangerous to attempt to use.

A basic tenant of survivalists is that training and skills are more valuable than stored supplies; largely they are right. It makes sense that training and skills become more and more important the greater the infrastructure damage. Damage compromises availability of external assistance. Rely on having basic supplies to stay alive and be able to use or barter with your skills.

Having a supply that is useful for a specific situation can save lives or simplify a task.

This page intentionally blank.

Notes: Where an Event Might Happen

Notes: Where an Event Might Happen

Chapter 6
Being Ready

Because there many different types of possible survival events, being ready often comes down to knowing what you have. If you use an inventory and a map you can find them, and any special instructions needed to use the supply, e.g., setting up a PV system.

A critical consideration is how to store and rotate stored supplies. Rotation is critical if supplies are perishable (e.g., water) or are time limited (e.g., batteries). How you store supplies determines useful life. How you store them includes control of things like temperature, humidity, insects, vermin, and moisture. Eliminating vermin access is difficult but necessary because vermin can chew through just about anything, ruining supplies they get into.

Organization and Storage Guidelines

Organizing your supplies can be challenging. The best organization is whatever works for you. The following guidelines will help:

Group supplies by function and size/weight.
Use large containers with handles.
Use durable containers but don't overload them.
Take pains to vermin proof the storage area.
Use a digital inventory but have a printed copy.
Keep a storage area map but have a printed copy.
Seal waterproof bags (usually only water-resistant).
Use sealed vacuum bags where appropriate.
Use desiccants in sealed bags or sealed containers.
Use container labels that don't fall off.
Label container contents and number the containers.
Label individual boxes in containers as needed.
Record purchase date and shelf-life on each item.
Use a permanent marker on a removable label.

Maintain accessibility to items that need rotating
Maintain access to items you might need in a hurry.
Maintain a reasonable speed of access to all items.
Keep storage areas locked, or at least not obvious.
Do disclose the inventory to a trusted person(s).
Don't disclose your stored supplies outside your family.
Don't disclose what you have to anyone.
Don't disclose supply location to anyone.

In many cases, you will need to duplicate a frequently used supply because you need to keep one with each functional grouping of supplies that may need it, e.g., duct tape. You need to maintain supply grouping since you might have an immediate need. One system uses plastic bins labeled by function, and then stores them in groups of similar use.

Some items are sealed (cardboard or paper packaging does not mean it is sealed). In some cases, if you leave them in its packaging, it may have a longer storage life. In other cases, you need to open the packaging to be able to inspect and test the item (e.g., if it uses plastic parts then it is probably not durable or reliable). Always attempt to inspect an item before storing it.

Other people will need to access supplies. Store a map of bin locations and bin contents with the supplies. Keep a digital file of the map and bin contents on a flash drive, in your EMP can (a Faraday cage). A computer search will identify the location of specific supplies. Repackage all items for long-term storage (e.g., purging air out of bulk grains that contain oxygen and humidity).

In cases where condensation is possible or humidity is often over 50% put insulating stand-offs under a storage container, e.g., wooden pallets. If the container holds organic supplies, like cloth, seal it after removing air and humidity. Put a drying desiccant in the container too.

Even if you believe the humidity source is clean and will not cause problems, don't take a chance.

An inexpensive desiccant is unscented silica gel cat litter. Put it in cloth tea bags in storage containers to dehumidify.

Pure water will not cause problems. Distilling water to make pure water occurs under controlled conditions, usually in a normal atmosphere. When exposing pure water to atmosphere that contains oxygen, water absorbs the oxygen. Absorbed oxygen causes oxidation problems with whatever the water contacts.

Pure or distilled water is rarely pure water since the distillation process usually takes place in an atmosphere that contains oxygen. Water absorbs oxygen. It is purer than tap water.

When an event has occurred, expect survivors to begin looking immediately for supplies they need to stay alive. They will try to convince you to share what you have. Your first priority is to maintain your health. Store supplies in a safe location. Survivors will become desperate for supplies and will resort to violence.

Make sure supplies are accessible to only your group and that you can defend them. It is unsafe to approach a locked location that others know contains supplies.

This does not apply to supplies you have hidden along a bug-out route. If you store supplies in remote locations, make sure only you can find them. Record an accurate location so others can retrieve remote supplies when necessary. If you store supplies in a freezer, e.g. antibiotics, record it on your storage map. If you use a safe, record the location of a written lock combination or key location on your supplies list.

It is unrealistic to store supplies far from your bug-in. If you store supplies remotely, you may not be able to get to them.

Medical Needs

Your first needs will be for medical supplies, shelter, and debris clearing tools. You cannot react to your own medical needs if incapacitated. Be sure that others have access to your medical supplies after an event has happened. Once healthy, you can help other survivors. Medical supplies will be the focus of intense envy and will attract people who want to take them.

Have a fully stocked medical kit ready. A medical kit must be ready at all times. Store it in a sealed vacuum bag with desiccants. The most often needed procedures will be stopping bleeding and treating burns. Severity and complications will govern applicable treatment. Include basic patient monitoring supplies in your kit.

Bandages, gauze, antibiotic creams, tourniquets, and pain relievers will be in high demand. Use them to treat the injuries of survivors as they clear debris. After initial treatment you need to monitor a patient to make sure he/she is comfortable and understands her/his situation and what you are or will be doing. You will create goodwill by addressing medical needs of others.

Take a wilderness first-aid course so you know how to assess a medical problem and know what to do (and when to do it). You can do more harm by attempting a medical procedure that you have not practiced. The best solution is to have a medical professional in your survival group. The next best solution is to know where one is available.

If the event extends there will be less water and food. Diarrhea will be common. If it affects you, you cannot defend yourself or your supplies. A diet of unfamiliar foods causes diarrhea and constipation. Use loperamide anti-diarrhea pills to lessen diarrhea. Eating high fiber foods also reduces constipation.

Unfamiliar foods increase the probability of eating something that is toxic or spoiled. It is best to carefully inspect and smell suspicious foods, even more so when hungry. A useful test is to offer the food to an animal. If they refuse it, you should too.

Electrical Needs

Expect electrical outages in survival events. Use a photovoltaic electrical system, a generator, or batteries for critical lighting and electronics. Tesla has a PV charged battery system for emergency power. It is expensive but it is a great alternative source of power.

A natural gas driven standby generator will be useless if line-pressurizing electrical compressors don't work. You may be able to run one on stored propane.

Use rechargeable batteries if you use them daily but use alkaline batteries while rechargeable batteries are charging. Stored rechargeable batteries lose charge over long storage periods. It is critical to have battery driven motion-sensing lights to alert you to intruders, so always have alkaline batteries available.

Rotate and replenish batteries. Rechargeable batteries lose most of their charge after five years and alkaline batteries after seven years. Both work after the replacement point, but not as well as when fresh. You can recharge dead rechargeable batteries so that they work again but realize that their charge is much less than alkaline batteries.

Never put a 7-volt lithium ion battery in a device designed to use 1.5-volt alkaline batteries. The higher voltage will probably destroy the device. Some lithium-ion batteries have identical AA alkaline battery dimensions.

There are premium and economy NiMH rechargeable battery choices, mostly AA. A good choice for premium rechargeable batteries is Panasonic Eneloop and for economy brands Amazon Basics. Use premium rechargeable batteries for applications that are intensive (greater battery drain) functions and economy brand rechargeable batteries for non-critical functions. AA batteries have a greater stored charge than AAA batteries.

Store alkaline batteries as a reserve for when you cannot recharge rechargeable batteries. They last longer than rechargeable batteries and can be stored for as long as 10 years; stored rechargeable NiMH batteries hold a usable charge for up to five years. Length of storage depends on temperature and humidity.

Use a battery voltage tester periodically to see if stored alkaline batteries still work. Use a rechargeable battery charge tester periodically to see if they still work. Rotate alkaline batteries as frequently as necessary to maintain a useful battery supply.

In a survival event, minimize your electrical power use. PV systems can meet this reduced usage need. PV systems have a low energy density, in other words they provide limited electrical power. Use battery bank electrical power storage systems to store power generated by PV systems. Typically, a 12-volt battery bank meets minimized demand. PV systems can be portable.

If you have a 12-volt battery bank use a battery tender to maintain it but replace the batteries every 5-7 years.

BOBs and BOPs

This is out of sequence but the subject of Bug Out Bags (BOBs) and Bug Out Packs (BOPs) needs consideration. Consider BOBs, Get Out of Dodge (GOOD) bags, and

I'm Never Coming Home (INCH) bags as the same thing. Although this book focuses on bugging-in, think about what it takes to leave a bug-in.

BOBs provide essentials to sustain you for up to two weeks. With foraging and scavenging, a BOP sustains you indefinitely. BOPs supplement BOBs. Neither bag has all the supplies you will need for an extended period. An example is drinking water, which is bulky and heavy to carry; a BOB would have containers you can fill and refill but the BOP should have a water filtration device.

You need to prepare one BOB, GOOD, or INCH bag for each adult member of your family, just in case. Adult, since having one depends on ability to manage its contents. They are for immediate grab-and-go situations (no time to rush around looking for items that should already be in the bag). Usually there is no one physically fit enough to carry a BOB very far. Use a cart.

The following pictures are of a game cart modified for carrying a BOB + a Sleep System (SS) or a BOB+SS+BOP plus event specific supplies. The cart method of travel hauls more, relieves physical strain and allows instant freedom of motion, as well as being able to navigate car clogged roads and off-road terrain.

Keep tarps and bungee cords stored with each cart to shield cart items from weather and from prying eyes. The downside is that you are walking but you can tow them behind a bicycle. Carts need to be sturdy enough to carry additional supplies and have solid rubber tires so they will not get a flat. Consider other designs that fit your needs. Here is an example of one:

Figure 8. Example cart used for bugging-out

There are steel wheels at the front. If you travel on roads or open country there will be objects that tear apart standard nylon or plastic wheels. The front height of the wheel support structure, levels the bed, and relieves pushing strain.

For many it is unrealistic to carry a BOB or BOP due to physical condition or weather. The probability of cold temperatures and winter weather is important. Hypothermia results from cold weather. Adequate cold weather sleeping systems are necessary since cold weather can happen without warning.

BOPs are large and even heavier than BOBs. Use them when a planned departure is possible. With foraging and scavenging, BOPs should sustain user(s) almost indefinitely. Carry them by vehicle, sled, or cart. Don't use carts on snow and ice,-use sleds. A strategy is to use a duffel bag with shoulder straps so you can move it around. If you plan to carry a BOB as a pack or even wheeled luggage (not a good idea), make sure you are fit.

To recap, BOBs are small and used for situations that have an immediate departure. BOBs should sustain the user up to 14 days. BOPs supplement BOBs. Use a BOP when you implement a planned departure from your bug-in. BOPs are larger and much heavier than BOBs. Plan to carry them by backpack, vehicle, sled, or cart. If you plan to carry a BOB as a pack or even wheeled luggage (not a good idea), make sure you are physically fit and that you reduce BOB size and weight to make it easier to carry.

The Aftermath

Dealing with the aftermath of an event will be exhausting. The greatest complication will be working with hysterical and panicked survivors. Know what you want to do and do not let spur of the moment suggestions from onlookers change your intent. Your first priority is to maintain your own health and safety so you will be able to provide assistance to others.

You may have to abandon survivors whose behavior threatens your safety or will not cooperate with you. An irrational person can cause a situation that harms you. Be as prepared to help others but also be prepared to walk-away. Walking away is emotionally tough but you will still be able to help someone else.

The aftermath of an event may include damaged infrastructure, e.g., roads, bridges, structures, and utilities. First responders will avoid using damaged infrastructure, making response time unpredictable. Most services will be unavailable. You can only depend on yourself, for your own needs and for helping others, when infrastructure is unreliable. Don't assume that first-responders will arrive or would help you.

Helping others could be anything from a physical rescue to providing an alternative to first-responders. You will need tools like chainsaws, pry bars, bow saws, jacks, rope (at least 50 feet of it – and strong too), dust masks, stretchers, and bracing timber for physical rescues. Later you will need things like flares, whistles, signaling mirrors, and smoke to attract rescuers. Depending on materials around you, you may be able to repurpose or improvise a signal that attracts help.

Notes: Being Ready

Notes: Being Ready

Chapter 7
Useful Skills

The most important supply is knowledge. Spend time practicing it; you can quickly apply knowledge as a skill. Medical and dental skills will be the most in-demand of any skill. Relieving suffering uses a different skill than setting bones, treating burns, or stopping bleeding.

Medical and dental skills are only useful if you have food, water, shelter, and self-defense supplies under control. You must be able to use them but that only happens when your situation is under control. You can push yourself so hard that you don't get adequate rest and jeopardize using medical or dental skills.

Lack of adequate sleep reduces your ability to exercise good judgment and planning, and that leads to accidents.

Dental problems are usually less critical than medical problems. If uncared for they can become painful or life threatening. Your best option is to have dental problems taken care of as soon as possible – you don't want a flare-up while you cope with a survival event. Stock-up on basic dental supplies and get a book on dental hygiene, like *Where There Is No Dentist*.

About 80% of injuries are sprains or soft tissue injuries. Viral and bacterial illnesses are about 60% of medical problems. Expect most of your medical response to focus on soft tissue issues (including infections).

Many sources offer training but you need to practice the training to be skilled. Many are free through the Red Cross. Volunteering as a wilderness medical resource is a way to get practice. Have at least two printed books (not eBooks) available to refer to.

Surgical skills will be in-demand for treating wounds. Having surgical skills means more than cutting and sawing. The training it takes to have effective surgical skills is difficult and detailed. Today, medical access is through the concentration of skills at hospitals and clinics.

Take heed of the physicians' creed, "Do no harm." It is easy to try performing a procedure that you have not practiced. If you do, you can easily have complications. The human body is resilient and can repair its self if given time and a supporting environment.

If there is no external assistance available and the alternative is death, then make the decision to use surgical procedures. Look for external assistance, even when the need is not immediate.

Using a landline telephone to request help determines exact location and help arrives quickly. Using a cellular phone, location is approximate and help arrives more slowly.

If you assume the role and responsibilities of medical or dental responder:

You are responsible for the patient. Inform the patient why you are treating him/her and what you are doing.

Act quickly and without apparent stress or indecision. Be calm because the patient will reflect it.

Stabilize the patient before you proceed. Immobilize him/her if necessary and stop any bleeding.

Protect yourself and the patient from infection from un-sterile supplies, or each other's diseases.

Do not attempt what you have not practiced, unless you are certain that the alternative is death.

Do not hesitate to allow a suddenly available experienced medical practitioner to take over.

Assemble your collection of medical supplies on your own, so you can take time to learn how to use each item (and how not to). Avoid most of the pre-packaged first-aid kits that are widely available. If you don't have time to assemble your own kit, use a quality camping kit and add to it.

You will need appropriate medical tools for common problems but there are far more medical tools than you can realistically learn to use correctly. This means that some problems are so severe that you risk making the problem worse by having and using tools that you think can do the job. Having the tools may be useful if you find someone who knows how to use them.

You can never have enough bandages. There are many types: adhesive, pressure, roll gauze, gauze pads, coagulant gauze, chest seals, sterile and non-sterile variants, burn dressings, broken bone slings, etc. For example, if you use two bandage changes a day for seven days before letting it scab over, you will use 14 bandages. Use fewer when treating a **minor** wound by bandaging it for only three days, before letting it scab-over.

Never get a patient's blood on your skin because disease is often absorbed through the skin or through cuts and abrasions.

Minor wounds need immediate attention to prevent infection. Disinfect and apply an antibacterial ointment (like bacitracin). After three days of keeping the wound bandaged, clean, and dry the antibacterial ointment will have done its work. Let the wound scab over from air exposure, to conserve bandages.

It is simple to treat most cuts if you have the necessary supplies. Apply direct pressure to the wound for several minutes to stop bleeding. Clean the wound with sterile distilled salt water and remove any wound debris. Let it bleed to help clean it out and apply a disinfectant to the wound, then to the surrounding area.

Before bandaging a wound, dry it by briefly placing sterile gauze on it. If the wound is extreme, pack it with sterile gauze to stop bleeding. After a two or three days carefully remove the packing. First, loosen dried blood by soaking the packing with warm sterile salt water and waiting while dried blood loosens.

Use butterfly strips, e.g., steri-strips, duct tape strips, or skin glue to close a minor wound. Use a skin stapler if it is major. Finally, bandage it carefully with a sterile gauze pad held in place by some type of sterile, or at least clean, bandage.

Do not use sutures to close a wound unless you know what you are doing and have at least practiced the procedure.

Puncture wounds infect quickly and result from things like clearing debris. Even if the object that caused the puncture is clean, germs on the skin move deep into the body. You should look closely at any object removed from the puncture wound to see if a small piece might have broken off inside the wound; remove it. After a few minutes, stop bleeding using pressure on the puncture. Clean the wound as you would clean a cut.

About twelve years ago, America's surgical mask makers moved operations overseas. America went from a 90% U.S. made mask supply to a 90% foreign made mask supply. When there is a sudden increase in global demand for surgical masks, like in a pandemic, it is likely that governments will stop mask shipments to foreign buyers. Store some in sealed bags, with desiccants to help prevent trapped moisture that deteriorates the masks.

The worst disease transmission vector is contact with bodily fluids. Even if you maintain your isolation by bugging-in, there will be times when you have no choice but to go outside your bug-in. A surgical mask or a respirator and gloves will help you stay isolated. Staying isolated not only protects you but gives those you come in contact with reason to not avoid you.

Transmission vectors for many diseases (e.g., Malaria, West Nile virus, Lyme disease, encephalitis, Zika) are insects and animals. These types of disease have more than tripled according to the CDC. It will only get worse as changing weather patterns and travel spread the range of insects. Add to this the possibility of new diseases resulting from melting permafrost and you have a high probability of new types of pandemics.

Knowing what might happen, and being ready for them, could prevent panic and doing the wrong thing at the wrong time. You could encounter many types of medical problems in a bug-in situation. Here is a quick overview of some that could be frequent:

hypothermia – #1 survival problem, a body is cold
hyperthermia – a body is too hot
dehydration – drinking an too little fluids
animal bites – puncture wounds/lacerations
puncture injuries – animal bites and debris clearing
lacerations – debris clearing, disease transmission
snakebites – painful puncture, there may be venom
gunshot wounds – people protect their survival
infections – from reduced hygiene and animal attacks
skin rashes and reactions from polluting chemicals
viral disease – don't use antibiotics
bacterial disease – use a full course of antibiotics
joint injuries – sprains and twisted limbs mostly
broken bones – from minor falls and impacts
crushed bones – from major falls and impacts

drowning – rushing or standing water from flooding
burns – from sunburn to 2nd degree or 3rd degree
poisonous plants – accidental ingestion or exposure
feet – rashes, infections, blisters, strains, lacerations,
swelling It is hard to overstate the importance of
good foot care. Infections from improper care are
painful and life threatening. Keep socks clean
and change them often.

It is difficult to tell the difference between viral and
bacterial infections. Examine the wound for clues. If a
fever sets in try to assess the speed of temperature
increase. A high speed of temperature increase often
means it is a bacterial infection. When in doubt use an
antibiotic but use it wisely and use the full course.
Unfortunately, bacteria are very adaptable. The overuse of
antibiotics has made many of them resistant.

Treatment of viral infections is difficult, mostly because
viruses are very small and reproduce inside cells. Viral
infections include the common cold, flu, coughs, measles,
mumps, chickenpox, etc. Overuse of antiviral and
antibacterial drugs has resulted in drug-resistant microbes.

How to recognize and treat common conditions takes
another book. Luckily, there are a number of books to use.
To avoid or deal with common medical problems, follow
precautions such as:

Know your limits and don't exceed them. This applies to
expectations of what others do.

Detect internal organ damage. Press the skin over a
suspect area; skin rigidity may mean organ bleeding.

Create shelter to protect from weather extremes. Use a
simple tarp, but anchor it to resist wind.

Create fire to keep warm, to cook, to scare off wild
animals, to signal, to repel insects, to see at night, to
improve morale.

Layer your clothing to dress for changing weather. This is also a flexible sleeping system and prevents hypothermia. Clothing is a limited form of shelter.

Disinfect water to prevent waterborne bacterial illnesses from incapacitating anyone. It progresses from general malaise to diarrhea to possibly fatal. When in doubt purify water and don't rely on purity assurances that could change.

Avoid the wrong equipment by considering the task before starting it and choosing equipment to handle likely problems. Equipment must be adequate, reliable, and functional.

Keep boots loosely laced when walking on flat land or uphill, but lace them tightly walking downhill. Lacing them this way eases bunion and blister pain and decreases foot damage.

Keep blades sharp. Cuts occur when a dull blade is used and it slips. Forcing a cut is poor judgment. Use a spare blade and sharpen all blades frequently.

Immobilize patients to minimize movement, which can make an injury difficult to treat or make it worse.

Watch responsiveness and lucidity to foretell developing problems in either a patient or someone who is near you. It is a good predictor of food poisoning and onset of illness.

Use medical triage to control emotional response. It is better to save many lives than to use excessive time and supplies to treat one person when time is limited.

Use preventive hygiene to minimize exposure to microbes.

Other skills will be useful, just not as much as medical skills. The nature of these skills tempts people to offer them as an extension of what they know. You may want to learn one or two skills so you can trade with them. At least you will be in a better position to judge if the work is acceptable.

Useful Skills to Learn	
laundry	canning
distilling and brewing	gardening
construction	Baby care
mechanical repair	leather working
small appliance repair	electrical repair
make candles and soap	teaching
plumbing	cooking
hunting and fishing	sewing
poultry maintenance	ammunition reloading
livestock care	carpentry
blacksmithing	sharpening
	communications

Notes: Useful Skills

Notes: Useful Skills

Chapter 8
Sometimes It Takes a Village

A saying attributed to Native Americans, "It takes a village to raise a child," can apply to surviving an L2/L3/L4/L5 event. Ignore all thoughts that you can survive very long on your own. You might have an injury, be ill or unconscious, need defensive assistance, or require help to get something done. Unfortunately, depending on a group also exposes you to transmitted disease.

Depending on yourself too much is a sure way to find out when there is something you cannot handle by yourself, often too late. You depend on services for mundane things like trash removal, utilities, sewage systems, and stoplights. When they are gone, you will need a support group for the many mundane tasks.

Try to have people in your survival group who demonstrate the necessary skills to perform tasks. That does not mean that everyone needs to specialize in a specific type of work, just that it is good to have those skills available. Daily repetition of tasks will reinforce knowing what to do, how to do it, and when to do it.

What this means is that you need to assemble your own village, or mutual support group. Know who will provide specific skills and let them know they can join your survival group when the time comes. This also means that other members can focus on stocking more skill specific supplies and not the in-general stuff.

Survival tasks often happen simultaneously. Tasks like collecting water, food, firewood, doing laundry, foraging, etc. will be time-consuming, monotonous, and never-ending. The fabled mountain men that lived in the Rocky

Mountains chose isolation but depended on coexisting and trading with Native Americans. Their life span was short.

How do you decide if short-term or long-term isolation is the right thing to do? The primary deciding factor is the extent you believe that you will need support. Think of all the tasks you will be responsible for and your stamina level. Isolation introduces life-threatening choices and decisions that you cannot walk back. Isolation is difficult and you will need support.

If you believe you are experiencing an L1/L2 event then think in terms of short-term isolation. You can expect aid in an L1/L2 situation because law and order will still exist. You can expect containment of chaos and panic, but not in an L3/L4/L5 event. If you are experiencing an L3/L4/L5 event, then think long-term isolation. Wide scale infrastructure damage and a panicking hysterical population will effectively limit access to all supplies.

For short-term isolation, all you need is basic supplies. For long-term isolation, you can decide to isolate yourself by sealing yourself in a cave or a bunker. For long-term isolation, you will need an extensive amount and variety of supplies. If your goal is short-term isolation, then expect external assistance to arrive and believe the event will be short-term.

If you want to survive either a short-term or a long-term event, realize that others will covet your supplies. Take advantage of this by offering desperate survivors supplies for tasks you need help with. Although the best course of action is to limit your activity outside your home, other survivors will eventually know you are there. Make it to their benefit to support you.

Holding onto your supplies will be difficult when you leave your bug-in location. Others might follow you to find out where there are supplies they can take. Try to stay unobserved if you need to leave your home. Take an indirect route back while checking to make sure no one follows you. If you are in a group, stay in the interior of the group and not on the edge where attacks happen. Do not assume group leadership; then you become a target.

Critical Isolation Supplies

What are critical supplies to maintain self-sufficient isolation?

- **Water**

    The most important supply is water. Without it, you will live about three days. If you store it, and you should, you avoid unknown dangers trying to get it. Use it to buy help for tasks you cannot start and finish on your own.

    Why is water so critical to maintain your body's health?

Water is a lubricant for cell membranes.
Water delivers dissolved nutrients to cells.
Water carries dissolved waste away from cells.
Water with electrolytes allows signals to travel the nervous system, enabling muscle control.

    These are key points about harvesting or foraging for water. Everyone in your group should know them, before they bring back water that disables the entire group:

Bottled water is your best source and it transports easily.
Bottled water can last a long time. Your group should use bottled spring water if you want to avoid chemicals.

Store bottled water in a cool dry place, away from sunlight, and not directly touching cement. Don't stack more than four cases.

Disinfect all water – boil, filter, or add chemicals

Never drink saltwater unless you distill it first.

Try not to drink urine. At most, you could try to drink it only three times. It is a source of toxins. Boiling it only kills bacteria and some viruses; besides, it smells.

Do not eat snow to rehydrate. Eating snow can lead to dehydration because your body heats and melts the snow, which can cause hypothermia. It could contain bacteria and other organisms. Melt snow first and then purify the liquid before you consume it.

You need water for cooking and hygiene.

Know what to avoid. **Think before you drink.**

Conserve water but don't go too far. Dehydration effects vary from lethargy, loss of alertness, headaches, to urinary problems. Do not eat a large amount of salty food.

- **Food**

    Next, you want to ensure that you can eat and stay healthy while you cope with survival. Scavenging food when survivors compete for anything edible will get violent. Use foraging and scavenging or long-term farming to supply food will be more productive when using multiple people. Because other survivors will want food, you can use any surplus you have to buy help that you need.

    Be careful about offering food to buy services. It is better to "pay" using packaged food than to share your meal table. Do not display extra food.

    Forget trying to hunt or fish, unless you live in a rural area away from travel routes. If you live in an urban or suburban area, you can expect open land or forest to be teeming with inexperienced, but armed, hunters and anglers. If you are not accidentally shot, anything you manage to bag or catch will become the focus of an effort to take it.

Farming uses toxic products. When farming safeguards are gone, expect increased toxins. What does it mean to survival food? It means that you need to be careful about what you scavenge, and store, e.g., seed grain is different from feed grain.

Most people can live up to a month without food. What is happening is that the body uses fat cells for "fuel." The process is ketosis. After the fat cells are used up the body begins using muscle cells for "fuel", called wasting away.

A balanced survival diet is not possible but your body needs a minimum amount of nutrients to maintain long-term health. Lack of a balanced diet leads to diarrhea and constipation, have medications available. There are problems that result from over-reliance on a single food, e.g., over-consumption of meat causes constipation.

A type of survival meal from stored canned food is a tomato-based soup. It uses a strong tomato taste to mask the taste of odd or strong tasting meats, like tuna fish or salmon. Use canned tomato paste or sauce and crushed or diced tomatoes with added canned vegetables and dried onion or dried garlic for more flavor, simmer with enough added water for the meal.

Following is a table of some foods to store. Store what you eat, not what you find a bargain on. Store the first six items if for short-term isolation. For long-term isolation, focus on adding items. Stocking the last item depends on your lifestyle.

Food Supplies Guidelines
Short-term
• Canned foods, especially salmon, tuna, vegetables
• Dried grains like white rice (avoid brown rice*), Dried beans, inexpensive source of protein
• Nutrient dense dried nuts* and honey**
• Peanut butter, inexpensive and stores well
• Trail mix and energy bars
Long-term
• Jerked meats, for long-term consumption
• Canned freeze-dried meals, longest storage life
Additional
• Coffee and instant coffee are quick mood boosters and good for morale. You can barter with it.

* avoid foods with oils that become rancid
** honey has properties that help healing

- **Shelter**

  Weather has always been one of the greatest survival challenges. Humans can survive about three hours without shelter if the weather is bad. Immediately build a temporary shelter, because the need may be sudden and unexpected. A shelter helps you avoid hypothermia. Learn how to build shelters.

  - Do not let building time keep you from erecting a temporary shelter, just in case.
  - Do not integrate a shelter with supplies storage in a way that hinders access to supplies.

    Build a temporary shelter to meet immediate needs but be ready to abandon it. Building the permanent shelter to meet long-term needs is time consuming. Position it to take advantage of natural surroundings that reduce build effort.

    Locate a shelter to support your gathering, farming, hunting, self-defense, and safety needs. Something like a dugout shelter at the top of a low hill with 360° of unobstructed views meets most needs.

Features to incorporate when building a shelter
locate it with a 360-degree unobstructed view
have a minimal profile
require minimal construction material
provide good insulation, insulation from ground too
incorporate ballistic protection
have a temperature-controlled storage area
put a floor in the medical area (reduces dust)
integrate ventilation, for both cooling and heating
include wind, rain, and snow mitigation

- **Self-Defense**

  After water, food, and shelter, the next most important survival item to have is some form of self-defense. A self-defense that keeps attackers away from you is vastly preferable to one that relies on their closeness.

  Relying on only you for self-defense is asking for problems. A support group is highly preferable. Self-defense can be as basic as knowing some form of hand-to-hand fighting system, having an intruder alert system, or having a simple weapon (e.g., a club or knife) to repel intruders:

Use force only when absolutely necessary.
Be ready to defend yourself from friends.
Prepare for death, emotional pleas, and lying.
Train for near, distant, and moving targets.
Move, attacking a moving target is hard.
Increase vigilance at night.
Run away if possible. Avoid injury.
Carry a concealed weapon for personal defense, where legal. Practice using it.
Use more than one type of alert system. A second or third will give warning of an intrusion if intruders discover and deactivate one.

- **First Aid**

  There is only one solution, a well-stocked first-aid kit. What does well-stocked mean? It means having additional supplies that meet a wider range of needs. Retail kits tend to use dated, limited, and questionable supplies. The estimated retail cost of a well-stocked survival first aid kit cost is at least $300. You can avoid much of that expense by building your own kit.

  Purchase an outdoor or camping first-aid kit and add to it. The biggest drawback to a pre-packaged kit is the amount of each supply. If used for a larger group then it is better to keep replacement supplies in a separate bin and later replenish kit supplies when using any.

  First-aid supplies usually have expirations that vary. Keep track of the expirations and replace them to maintain their usefulness. Expired bandages may not be sterile and adhesives lose stickiness. Packaging fails so repackage supplies when it is failing.

  Even better, build your own medical kit and learn what works. Building one keeps expense down and it controls the amount of each component.

  Putting together you own kit lets you customize it to group needs and lets you understand how to use each item. A bin is useful to store less used items that are necessary for your group. Book Two goes into detail about possible medical kit contents.

- **Hygiene**

  You need good hygiene to stay healthy. It keeps you from getting an infection or catching a disease, common problems in a survival situation. There will be outbreaks of diseases that we thought were gone, because other survivors do not practice good hygiene. Good hygiene prevents medical intervention and the supplies it uses.

Loss of a water supply has greater consequences than hydration and cooking. Water powers the sewer system and lets you clean microbes from your skin. Water also cleans microbes and grit from living and cooking areas. Water is necessary for medical procedures. When it is limited, you must be creative in finding substitutes.

Use only clean water in food preparation. Lack of clean water causes gastrointestinal illness, infections, and disease. You may believe that boiling or long-term heat exposure will kill microbes but they easily re-enter food.

Recommended Hygiene Supplies	
dental floss	soap (lots of it)
detergent	wet wipes
diapers	HD garbage bags
surgical/facemasks	hand sanitizer
feminine supplies	clean clothes
shampoo	cleaning supplies
toothbrushes	toothpaste

Implementing and practicing good hygiene is critical to a healthy daily life. It takes diligence and attention to detail. Even the slightest lapse in hygienic practices could result in consequences that compromise your survival.

In a survival situation, microbes, viruses, and disease will be impossible to avoid. Try to avoid contact with them. This means you should at least wear disposable gloves and if necessary wear a disposable covering, like a smock, or clothes that can be quickly removed and laundered.

Surgical masks

There are two types of filtering facemasks, surgical and dust. Surgical facemasks only prevent direct germ transfer, like in coughing. You use a surgical facemask to limit germs and particulates from getting in your lungs. Use them for casual medical needs, not for things like dust or airborne toxins.

To filter out dust and airborne disease use something like the 3M Cool-Flow respirator. This type of mask is more efficient than surgical or dust masks and comes with an exhale valve. An exhale valve lets the mask pass an illness spread by airborne particulates. If this is a concern, masks like the PD-101 Full Face Organic Vapor Respirator are an alternative.

Use respirators with no exhale valve when you want to contain disease spread. Yours or the patient's illness may be mild but if the disease may not be mild if communicated to someone else. If working with a highly communicable disease, use respirators with no exhale valve for both you and a patient.

A benefit of using a respirator with no exhale valve during the winter is that your nose mucus membranes stay moist and able to block viruses and microbes. Actually, mucus membranes dry out when there is low humidity at any time. Technically, you need to maximize relative humidity. Use a night humidifier while you sleep to help stop airborne microbes.

The National Institute for Occupational Safety and Health (NIOSH) certifies the filter material of these masks. Two types prevent inhalation of particulates, N95 and N100 facemasks, where N indicates NIOSH approval. N95 masks filter out 95% of particulates and N100 masks filter out 100% of particulates, but those figures assume a complete face seal.

Plastic trash bags

Include heavy-duty plastic trash bags in a hygiene kit. Only your imagination limits their uses. Plastic trash bags are available in varying thicknesses, stock all of them since thicker bags compromise some uses.

Uses for Heavy-Duty Plastic Garbage Bags	
rain protection	temporary clothing
make a rope	gloves or shoes
make a sling weapon	collect unclean items
bandage wrap	temporary shelter
showering	plug shelter drafts
emergency tourniquet	hold insulation
broken arm sling	seal doors and windows
gill net for fishing	transport stuff
emergency flotation	emergency toilet
make a bed and pillow	prevent hypothermia

Laundry

We often overlook the impact of having clean clothes. The spaces in a weave trap grit and bacteria. Grit wears down fibers and often has an odor that gives away your presence. Disease carrying grit can cause infections. Keep clothes clean and wash your body often. Sponge bathe to reduce transferring skin grime to clothing and to conserve water.

- **Air Quality**

    After securing basic needs for water, food, first aid, hygiene, and shelter you can consider other needs. The most prominent is making sure that you are breathing good quality air. You can survive about three minutes without air. **Depending on the event, this may become your highest priority need.**

An allergic reaction or excessive/volcanic dust, is a survival situation. Wear a medical bracelet that tells others about allergies you have that might compromise your ability to breathe. There are portable oxygen kits you can use.

In most events, you will need to clean up debris and rescue others. Performing these can expose you to many hazardous substances; think of what happened to first-responders at the September 11, 2001 Twin Towers attack. Fires consumed all flammable materials, releasing chemical compounds as gases.

Chemical compounds are in smoke. These contaminants often cause both immediate and long-term health issues. The bottom line is that you should avoid the smoke of burning buildings, or even wood smoke, in a survival event. To avoid breathing gases use a full-face respirator and oxygen bottle or a full-face gas mask that uses fresh (not depleted) activated charcoal.

Facemasks do not filter out chemicals unless particulates, like dust or ash, carry them. You can put petroleum jelly on a beard to get a dust mask to seal to your face. Another sealing technique is to tape mask edges to your face.

Dust and ash from smoke and crushed cement will be common in survival events. Volcanic dust is damaging because it is sharp crystallized rock. If you cannot get out of the dust area, use a facemask (review information in Chapter 7) to remove most dust from what you breathe. Realize though that no facemask is 100% efficient at removing particulates. Stay inactive as much as possible.

In Summary

The key point in any survival situation is to be ready to provide your own support for any of these basic needs. Providing your own support depends on the type of survival event. Consider an event's intensity and its probable duration. Also consider the probability of external assistance and whether the situation is stable. Providers of external assistance will reconsider entering the event area if the event is unstable.

Too often people convince themselves that external assistance is imminent or that event intensity will subside. They believe it is safe, so they take foolish actions (like drinking too much of their water or eating too much of their available food). External assistance rarely happens the way expected and may not happen at all. Stay prepared until there is no doubt that external assistance has arrived and that it is addressing your needs.

This page intentionally blank.

Notes: Sometimes It Takes a Village

Notes: Sometimes It Takes a Village

Chapter 9
Likely Events

The purpose of this chapter is to re-emphasize precautions you can take. It reviews, consolidates, and adds detail to prior information. If you believe you understand the subjects and don't need more detail or subject matter repetition then you can skip this chapter.

The top priority for anyone is to stay alive. Few people would willingly give up their lives for someone else. The prior chapter explored basic needs of self-sufficiency. This chapter looks at specific actions you need to take in order to preserve and extend your life in some of the most probable survival events. You should modify the recommendations to fit the situation.

There are some common realities for all survival events. Expect and be prepared to deal with:

unreliable fuel, food and drinking water
unreliable utilities e.g., power, gas, water, sewage
unreliable services, e.g., trash pickup, sewer systems, firefighting, medical help, law enforcement.
neighbors and friends who want you to share
looters who will harm you or your group
being unsafe when outside your bug-in

Top 10 Survival Supplies

At minimum, you should have the following ten items to cope with at least L1/L2 survival events. Size each to fit your group. Rotate your stored food and water as needed. Use these for all events and add supplies specific to events you anticipate.

Remember that these are the minimum necessary and that additional supplies will be necessary as aftermath needs become clearer. Even with these basic supplies, realize that aftermath length determines minimum quantities of each.

1	short-term food and water
2	portable shelter
3	filtering water pitcher, with extra filters
4	a weather alert radio with battery backup
5	medical (first-aid) kit, with extra basic supplies
6	knives for utility use, and food preparation
7	flashlights and a lantern, with extra batteries
8	plastic trash bags (medium and heavy-duty thickness)
9	EDC kit and a GHB to help you get to a bug-in
10	BOB and BOP if forced to evacuate your bug-in

Consider getting a radio channels scanner to stay informed of first responder activity. It will help you deal with rumors and you can act as needed. There are additional details for each of these basic supplies in Book Two of the *Plan to Survive* series.

Even when first responder services are available, they could stop abruptly. Depending on the situation, your best bet will be to use available supplies to stabilize the situation until first responders are available. In all cases, you absolutely need to have an All Hazards Weather Alert radio to stay aware of developments. It picks up broadcasts of emergency information in addition to weather alerts.

Additional Critical Survival Supplies by Event Type

Assess the probability that the event will extend. Consider how it might change. Each of the following L2 event topics is a standalone section that refers to critical additions, which tend to be common to many events but need repeating in each stand-alone section. Think of them as representative of that type of event.

Survival depends on recognizing severity, intensity, probable aftermath duration, and event changes. Strategies for surviving one event are often applicable to other events. There are subtle changes in the priority of what to acquire to help you get through various events, based mainly on timing of need.

The probability does not matter as much as the potential each has for inflicting pain and suffering. Included with each are suggested survival strategies and supplies. Consider these in terms of what is likely to happen where you live.

1 Extreme Weather

Extreme weather is often the result of a changing climate. Recorded human history is brief when compared to the time the planet has existed with an environment that supported life. The effects of the changing climate that we experiencing are within the range this planet has seen. Environmental changes are difficult to live in until they stabilize.

Increased flooding, hurricanes, tornadoes, wildfires, blizzards, rainstorms, and windstorms will be unexpected because we expect historical weather patterns. In the stabilization time there will be droughts, prolonged cold weather, extreme seasons, species extinction, etc. with which to cope.

Impacts may be unexpected but we still need to cope with consequences. Human nature is to maintain an expected rhythm of living, even when disrupted by unexpected events. Adapt your lifestyle to survival because you will have limited access to just about everything. Access limitations will be minimal at first but will grow over time.

Stored supplies will help you cope with changes. They cannot sustain your lifestyle indefinitely. Their primary purpose should be to give you a chance to survive. You may be able to resume your lifestyle if you have survived the disruption.

You need to store the amount of supplies needed to cope with event aftermath, not for just an immediate need. Because extreme weather events seem to be more frequent, consider storing supplies that allow you to survive in two back-to-back events, when you have no time to resupply.

What can you do?

Depending on how widely spread disruption is, you can use options to reduce the impact. Consider what the common realities at the beginning of this chapter. Then review the list of basic supplies considering what is common in your area. Survival has priority but more supplies mean more comfort.

The most useful action to take is to store fuel (in a controlled location, with stabilizer added), subject to insurance and local regulations. In all L2 events fuel, water, and food shortages cause the most problems. Of those, fuel is the more critical item because with it you can leave to find what you need. Assess the probable length of the aftermath because that is what will determine what you should allow for fuel use.

A problem leaving an area affected by the extreme weather event is that the road system may be unreliable. The road system will be one of the first pieces of infrastructure repaired because bringing in supplies for survivors will be a priority. It is likely that the highway patrol will limit civilian traffic so trucks bringing in supplies don't experience delays. Another problem may be that looters could be hiding along the road.

Expect an extreme weather survival event to be brief and that there will be aid. Expect long-term aftermath challenges. FEMA says to have a 72-hour kit of supplies ready. You probably need at least one to two weeks of supplies to deal with the aftermath, not just the event. More people face death due to aftermath consequences than from the actual event.

There is extensive guidance for dealing with extreme weather. The problem is that, as climate patterns change uncommon weather will become more common. Prepare for the impact of increased rainstorms, flooding, cold weather, snow, and ice. Don't get caught in a situation where the local weather forecast is misleading, because it is using historic data.

2   Electrical Grid Failure

Electrical grid failure is usually a cascading event that affects interconnected but independent electrical power operating systems. There are three main electrical grid interconnection systems in the United States lower 48 states: Western, Eastern, and Texas. They are independent of each other.

The Eastern electrical grid interconnect system is sub-divided into major operating units that are also mostly independent of each other; SERC in the southern area, MRO in the Midwest area, Reliability First in the northeast area, FRCC in Florida, SPP in the southwest area, and NPCC in the northeast area. Theoretically, the effects of a problem in one will not cascade into an adjacent operating unit.

Any electrical grid problems from a CME or cyber-mischief event should be contained by the electrical grid interconnects. EMP or cyber-mischief events will likely affect multiple grid operating units. A CME event may affect a wide area. Cyber-mischief causes as much damage and panic as possible. Every electrical grid has multiple possible points of failure and causing a failure in one or more can spread the effects.

How widespread disruption of the electrical grid by a CME or EMP event is varies based on strength and range of the CME or EMP. Effects from one operating system should not cascade into adjacent operating units. A cyber-mischief event could target multiple operating units. An EMP example is the low or high-altitude atmospheric detonation of a nuclear device.

No known terrorist group has the capability of a high-altitude nuclear detonation but several nation-states do. Low-level detonation affects only electrical grid operating systems near it, in the line-of-sight. Society depends on electricity, when it is unavailable; it affects every function. The purpose of a terrorist group is to create fear and panic.

Mundane things like no traffic lights or no street lighting will cause disruption to a smoothly running infrastructure. Many stores have automatic doors that will cease to work. Expect locked stores as managers try to avoid looting. As disruptions multiply, there will be collateral disruptions. Don't become dependent on having electricity but learn alternative ways that don't use electricity to accomplish what needs to be done.

What can you do?

First, have the basic supplies listed at the beginning of this chapter. Depending on how widely spread it is, there limited options you can use to reduce the impact. The best response is to run a portable or a stand-by generator (and have fuel to run it). The next initial response is to avoid the main roads and get home.

Next, take stock of and consolidate what you have. Be one of the first to buy more food and water, preferably at a local store to avoid dangerous congestion. Panic buying by the general population will quickly strip available products from store shelves and make going to a store risky. Your best bet is to keep your pantry stocked with food (and keep it rotated).

Try to get more food and water, and any missing supplies, immediately. Trade excess food for something you need. If you hesitate too long realize that trying to buy food and water will become dangerous. Buy medical supplies that you can trade. Alleviating pain and suffering will always be in demand, especially medication for children.

Depending on how widespread electrical grid failure is, expect repairs to begin quickly. Don't make the same type of mistake that Puerto Rico hurricane survivors made. They started loading a repaired grid too quickly, causing further damage, and delays. Your best bet is to be able to rely on electrical power alternatives, e.g., PV systems or batteries. Parts availability will limit what repair crews can do.

In an urban setting, one of the biggest problems will be non-working traffic lights. Traffic light controlled intersections will become grid-locked and dangerous. Panicked motorists will cause chaos and confusion.

3   Cyber-mischief

Cyber-mischief uses Internet connectivity to spread malicious software. It activates when specific conditions exist or at a specific time. Perpetrators can even infect systems not directly connected to the Internet. They often use temporarily connected devices with programs that link to malicious software but that appear benign to detection programs.

It is likely that you will hear about individual effects to a limited number of systems over a period. Perpetrators may be testing the effectiveness of their penetration programs. Perpetrators could later unleash one or more simultaneous system infections. Watch for this type of activity and use awareness to fine-tune your estimate of attack probability.

The intent of a cyber-attack is usually to compromise specific systems. There is a wide range of possible targets but usually major affects appear first in the margins. Think of this as a sort of early warning system that you can monitor. Impending cyber-mischief might become apparent by watching for early effects. Usually these effects appear to be inconsequential.

Problems increase when computers control critical systems. Computers control systems like electrical compressors for gas transmission, routing, and scheduling. Expect refineries, banks, and utilities to stop working. When those become undependable, you will see a cascade of other problems When there are dependent systems, computers will shut down.

Notice that computer systems that involve fulfilling consumer needs are critical. Consumers are the general population and their mass reaction magnifies an impact. If they are inconvenienced any over-reaction will overstate the impact of cyber-mischief. One favorite trick is to use weather or financial disruptions to trigger cyber attacks.

Consider what happens when fuel or food is limited. Reduction drives a population to buy-up available products. There is panic when there is no longer product availability. Although food and fuel are the first products to sell out, medical supplies and camping gear soon follow. Your best bet is to spend the time you have gathering medical and camping supplies. Later you can trade them.

Financial system attacks are a indicator. Problems there often precede other attacks. Financial institution precautions will affect you even if a cyber-attack is behind the scenes. Typical precautions include stopping all electronic transactions. Because financial institutions need human interaction, system problems will create long delays while humans react.

With electrical power disruption, services will be sporadic and unreliable. Lack of electricity will limit your access to everything. The best action is to store fuel. Having fuel will allow you to run a generator and let you run your car so you can get to alternative services. Extra fuel will be a valuable commodity to barter.

Keep in mind that once a cyber-attack begins it could affect any system at any time, even when physically disconnected from the Internet (so-called air gap isolation). Cyber-mischief could result from a dormant program that does not activate immediately or from using a USB drive. Malicious software is getting ever more capable. It can even mimic trusted software. There is no complete defense.

The Internet (including the web and the dark web) is the weapon of choice for terrorists. Nation-states aid terrorists to release malicious software that is hard to trace back to the nation-state. A favorite attack is for malicious software to watch data flow and to activate on specific use patterns, on a specific date, or on command. Otherwise, it continues to hide from detection programs. Cyber attacks are just beginning.

What can you do?

Favorite targets are the electrical grid, Internet, and communications systems because their disruption causes panic. It is simple to disrupt cellular networks that relay cell phone conversations by overloading them with fake communications or confusing the computers doing the routing.

> Cell phones use computer networks to route calls. Have a landline in case cell phones are unreliable.

Often perpetrators use the justification "You did it, so we can too." Discontinue using websites or software known to track or watch you. It is likely those sites or software will b de the target of malicious software that will make your life difficult. For example, many websites use excessive tracking cookies.

Another precaution is to keep a reserve of cash in your house to use if financial or banking systems become unstable. If you use the Internet to make payments, know the phone numbers for customer service and numerical addressees where you can send payments. Have stamps and envelopes and ask financial institutions to start sending you paper billing statements.

A target for cyber-mischief is the Domain Name System (DNS). A DNS allows you to type easy-to-remember word addresses instead of number addresses. Use something like "Online URL-IP Converter" to build a list of numeric addresses for each word URL you use.

A good practice is to disconnect your computer from the Internet when not using an Internet function. Reconsider using connected (through the Internet "cloud") devices. Web-connected devices are often the target of cyber-mischief. Recently cyber-mischief perpetrators used cloud-connected video cameras to launch a DNS attack on the DNS system, briefly disrupting part of the web.

Most personal computer hacking involves getting into a computer through the browser. Often infected JavaScript software runs automatically when you link to a site. Site owners are usually not aware that malicious software uses their site. Use an extension to the Firefox browser called "NoScript." It prevents JavaScript programs from running unless you specifically authorize the program to execute.

4 Pandemics

Pandemics have roughly the same impact as cyber-mischief because systems use human interaction. When an individual is sick, systems are not able to maintain human interaction. Expect increased absences to result in reduced services.

The effect of operators being ill is to make a system unreliable. The main difference to a cyber-mischief event is that a pandemic will be larger scale. Illness will spread and all systems may become unavailable. Expect mundane things like sewage, trash removal, and ATMs to be unreliable.

At first, expect a localized illness. If it spreads, it becomes a regional epidemic. When the region it is active in expands significantly, it becomes a pandemic. If it reaches widespread regional activity, it gets attention but that may be too late. When it spreads globally, it is a global pandemic.

Vaccine development is a long slow process. Unless the disease got out of a lab where a vaccine is ready, isolation becomes the only practical near-term means of coping.

There is speculation as to the source of the next pandemic. It will probably be a virus and viruses are hard to defeat. You need to use a drug that specifically targets the virus. Even then, you must use it so that it does not mutate into a form resistant to a vaccine.

Most scientists believe the next pandemic will be from an existing virus, probably mutated. Flu mutates frequently, which is why the vaccine changes every year. The 1918 flu mutated and killed 5% of people on this planet. It infected people already weak from fighting off the previous strain.

The leading candidates for a pandemic virus could be a virus released by melting permafrost or a mutated existing virus. It is even possible that it will be a space borne pathogen, using a totally unknown chemistry. If it is a space borne virus, it may be an L5 event.

The World Health Organization (WHO) has a system of phases to identify the status of flu spread:

Phase 1	No new influenza virus has been found.
Phase 2	A new virus appeared in animals, but there are no cases of transmission to humans.
Phase 3	The strain of animal virus identified in Phase 2 infects humans, but there have not been human-to-human infections.
Phase 4	The virus passes from person to person, but transmission is limited and confined.
Phase 5	There is frequent transmission of the virus between people in a specific place, but it has not spread beyond a known area.
Phase 6	Pandemic. The virus spreads worldwide. A vaccine is not yet available.

Our normal defenses may be useless because they are location oriented. Insects and animals migrate to new areas based on food supply. When they migrate, they bring diseases with them. Animals (including humans) often have no defense against these new diseases, e.g., the Zika virus or West Nile virus.

What can you do?

Your best defense against a microbe is to stay isolated and breathe filtered air. Viruses are generally so small that most filters, even high efficiency particulate air (HEPA) filters, will not filter them out. The good news is that viruses usually attach themselves to larger particles that you can filter out.

Consider clean rooms to change HEPA filters without exposing yourself to contaminated air. Whole house HEPA filtering systems are available and can be cost effective if you use forced air heating or whole-house air-conditioning. In a pandemic, use non-porous gloves to remove and replace HEPA filters. Disinfect gloves when finished. Place used filters in a plastic (non-porous) bag and seal it shut.

There are many forms of virus transmission. A virus could be air borne or water borne; it could infect animals and transmit from them to humans. HEPA filter air you breathe and sanitize surfaces and objects exposed to contamination. The most effective means of transmission is contact with other survivors, even at a distance. **Maintain isolation**.

Virus mutation and infected area information changes rapidly. Listen to your portable, battery backed-up, All Hazards Weather Alert radio for updates. Acting in a timely manner to breaking contagion news could save your life. Consider relocating if contagion spread appears to be moving toward your location. Wait until virus activity "burns-out."

Did you know that we created Ellis Island in order to stop the spread of disease? Although this was a drastic measure, it may be necessary again. Temporary traveler quarantine and isolation may work. There has been some success using this to combat the current pandemic. Another pandemic is certain.

5   Financial or Social Collapse

Crime increased when Argentina's economy collapsed. Rapes went up 165%, car thefts climbed 248%, robberies increased 4159%, aggravated assaults rose 5597%, and burglaries went up by 512,100%. Argentine society still has not recovered and social unrest continues. Now it is happening in Venezuela.

The U.S. economy almost collapsed on 9/17/2008. Investors withdrew $140 billion from the money market. If withdrawals had continued, the economy would have collapsed. If a collapse affects local governments and utilities, then water and electricity would no longer be available.

As people panic, they revert to survival and self-defense. This leads to a collapse of linked mutually dependent systems. Financial or social collapse is a series of inter-related conditions, like a line of dominoes falling. The effects of collapse will last at least a year. Considering that, the aftermath length will make recovery difficult.

Financial or social collapse has effects similar to a pandemic. Knowing there will be no paycheck, people would do their job without enthusiasm or attention to detail, or not go to their jobs at all. For a glimpse of what this might be like in the United States consider effects of the recent federal shutdowns.

There is strong probability that an event like this will trigger rioting. How a collapse event plays-out varies from a minor inconvenience to a complete overhaul of financial and political systems. If authorities realize their tenure is in jeopardy they will react. If a collapse is rooted in perceived social injustices then expect a long stabilization period.

What can you do?

A prudent option is to have fuel. We base much of our lives on being able to use services. If a riot disrupts this, you will need a way to ensure you can access critical services. Having fuel will allow you to use a car to leave an area. Rioting tends to burn itself out so staying in your home and blocking entry will give you time to wait-out rioting.

Your best defense against the effects of an event like this is to store food, water, and medical supplies. Since riots will be the most probable danger, stock additional supplies to cope with that type of event.

Supplies that give you the ability to remain out-of-sight of a riot mob will be invaluable.

Limit travel away from home because you don't want to encounter a riot, but also because you don't want to lead anyone back to your home. Stay away from a riot unless you know its nature and intention. Riots are rarely organized. They often change focus, making them act unpredictably. Sometimes a riot acts at crossed purposes. Monitor your TV and radio for information as to riot scope or expectations.

Be ready to act in self-defense, when traveling or at home. Carry a concealed pistol if you have a permit (do not wave it around because the police see that as threatening). Police take a dim view of citizens using deadly force. Have non-lethal crowd control available so you can use a non-lethal form if you need to. Sweep the front of an advancing crowd.

Use a sub-compact 9MM pistol for concealed carry but a .45 caliber pistol for home defense. A .45 bullet hits with more energy and is more accurate (longer barrel).

Use #6 or #7½ birdshot in a pistol grip 20-gauge shotgun to stop a crowd. Use two shotguns, one active, and one reloading. Birdshot only causes pain at 30 yards but bleeding at 10 yards and is lethal at four yards.

Expect destructive riots so store a supply of facemasks and goggles (to limit smoke and tear gas effects). In addition, store basic medical supplies, temporary toilets, fire extinguishers, and cash (since banks and ATMs will not work). It is a big assumption to think that law enforcement authorities and other emergency services will be active.

Note the location of cash on your supplies map in case someone else needs to use it. Do not advertise the location of, or that you even have, cash.

These are leading financial indicators to watch. If they simultaneously signal a collapse is imminent, be extra alert to further changes and start stocking up on supplies:

Monitor the financial markets. Big market changes often signal a looming major financial decline.

Follow the fluctuations of precious metal prices. An unexplained spike in values often means that other investors foresee a major event.

Watch 10-year bond yields. Rising yields indicate that investors are shifting money out of the stock market. This happens when confidence in the value of stocks is low.

Watch commodities. If prices drop, expect inflation and a slow economy. If prices rise, inflation increases.

Pay attention to oil prices. If oil prices are decreasing, expect all financial markets to decline.

Watch precious metal prices. If they increase significantly then financial institutions expect a stock market collapse.

Have cash at your home (nothing larger than a $20 bill). Cash has value only if there is confidence in the issuing authority. Assess how long government control will last or whether it might be re-established. Pay bribes in untraceable cash, while control lasts. If the event is severe, cash may not hold its value

Inflation is a consequence of a printing (fiat) currency to pay debt. Fiat currency has value based only on a promise to pay. Governments use fiat currency to pay interest. Many people believe that governments are moving toward financial collapse because they depend on fiat currency.

6 Seismic Activity

Seismic activity is both induced and naturally occurring. Induced seismic activity is generally only a minor occurrence right now (think of hydraulic fracturing fluid disposal or sequestering carbon dioxide).

Manipulating and amplifying induced seismic activity is a major area of research. There is concern that an induced seismic event could trigger a tsunami.

Most natural seismic activity occurs where tectonic plates meet, like the Pacific Rim. The greatest seismic event in the history of this planet was in the middle of a tectonic plate. Frequency of even the smallest earthquakes can predict activity. The United States Secretary of the Interior said he is accelerating placement of earthquake detection sensors along the U.S. west coast, as part of an effort to predict activity.

In addition to collapsed buildings and damaged infrastructure, expect landslides and liquefaction. Liquefaction is the phenomenon in which solid ground acts like a fluidized solid. Shaking, landslides, and liquefaction will cause fires, flooding, pipe breaks, hazardous material spills, etc., and an increased loss of life. If you are near the coast, a tsunami would cause even more damage and death.

There is measurement for earthquakes, the Richter scale. A 30-second earthquake generally has a Richter scale measurement in the mid-sevens. A minute-long quake is in the high sevens. A two-minute quake is in the eights and a three-minute quake is in the high

eights. By four minutes, an earthquake has hit
magnitude 9.0. Unfortunately, the Richter scale
cannot predict earthquakes-nothing does, yet.

What can you do?

This type of situation can cause a variety of effects.
The electrical grid will fail soon after the shaking
begins. People who are home when it hits should be
safe. The first problem will be transporting and
distributing fuel, food, and water. Expect utilities and
services to be unreliable. We depend on electricity so
if a seismic event disrupts availability you will need
an alternative. A useful option is a generator.

If you live in a seismically active area, keeping
supplies in one location is risky. They could be
isolated from you, buried, trapped in a collapsed
building, burned in an area fire, soaked and unusable,
etc. Divide supplies among storage locations or store
an emergencies canister remotely. Store it within a
one day walking distance (probably less because
damage may slow you down). Keep a backpack in the
canister.

Your best defense is to store survival food, water, and
medical supplies. You can expect many toppled trees
blocking access routes and the need to rescue others
from damaged buildings. This means, at minimum,
you will need tools, at least 50 feet of strong rope,
dust masks, gloves, and a hard hat. Other tools you
will need to deal with the aftermath:

- chainsaw (with extra chains, oil, and fuel)
- at least two long crowbars and a shovel
- jack (to lift debris that is heavy or hard)
- long metal pry bar to move heavy debris
- sledge hammer (to break up debris)

- long tube with a funnel (water to trapped victims)
- bracing lumber (for supporting structures)
- first-aid kit and tourniquets to stop bleeding

Store the basic supplies listed at the beginning of this chapter. In addition, store facemasks and goggles (to limit smoke and dust effects), more basic medical supplies (since debris will injure many), temporary toilets, and fire extinguishers.

Basic earthquake survival rules:

Drop, take cover, and hold on (something sturdy).
In a building, expect fire alarms and sprinklers.
Avoid windows. When glass breaks, shards spray.
Avoid bookcases or furniture that can fall on you.
In bed, hold-on, stay there, and protect your head.
Stay indoors until the shaking stops.
If outdoors, avoid buildings, trees, and power lines.
Have the right tools to turn off your utilities.
If driving: go slow, go to a clear area, and stay in it.
Make your home sturdier by attaching to wall studs.
Know a safe place in each room to take shelter.
Learn evacuation routes where you live and have locations where family members go to reunite.

7   Tsunamis

Of all the natural disasters, tsunamis are the biggest killers, and the most terrifying. They can result in a wall of water as much as 100 feet high. Even when they recede, they create an undertow. The only way to survive is to be somewhere else.

You have only 2-4 minutes of oxygen in your lungs. Do not think you can swim or float, there are strong currents and under-tows. Floating debris is deadly. Even a strong swimmer cannot swim out of a tsunami.

Tsunamis happen when there is a shift in the depth of
water or a coastal landmass collapses into the sea. The
displaced water moves as a swell on the surface of the
body of water, creating a downward force. Because of
this force, even being underwater when the tsunami
passes will not insulate you from damage by the
tsunami. Submarines have reported violent
movements when a tsunami swell passed.

When the swell and force reach shallow water, the
downward force partially reflects off the seabed and it
becomes higher. When it reaches dry land, it contains
all of the displaced water because the downward force
reflects fully. The swell travels over dry land until the
combination of friction with the land surface and
height of the land dissipates the swell.

Tsunamis are killers, even if you survive an earthquake.
The Indonesia tsunami in 2004 killed over 250,000
people. The magnitude 9.0 Tōhoku (Japan) earthquake
and tsunami killed over 20,000. The tsunami caused
most of the 20,000 Tōhoku deaths. FEMA believes that
there will be over 15,000 deaths in a Cascadian
earthquake and tsunami in the NW U.S.

Whoever lives through a tsunami will spend 3-6
months without electricity and use bottled water for 1-
3 years. There will be no sewage systems and no
hospitals. It takes replacement equipment, time,
money, and skilled labor to reconstruct damaged
infrastructure. Think of how long Puerto Rico is
taking to restore electrical power, even partially.

Ankle-deep water moving at only 6.7 miles an hour
can knock over an adult.

What can you do?

Tsunami warning systems monitor the ocean surface for swells that don't meet the criteria of waves. A swell can dissipate in the ocean but when it is large enough it travels until it reaches dry land. When it reaches land, the volume of water is a tsunami. The force of water traveling at the speed a tsunami propagates is significant.

A tsunami causes a wide variety of effects but the actual event is brief. The event may be brief but the aftermath is not. Your best bet is to store supplies that assume long aftermath duration. Since a tsunami is a coastal event, expect external aid from unaffected inland sources.

The biggest problem will be gathering, transporting, and distributing fuel, water, and food because damaged roads and other infrastructure are not safe or not reliable. Expect utilities and services to be unreliable. Listen to your radio for current information.

Basic tsunami survival guidelines

If you see a tsunami, you are too close. Shaky ground, water receding, and a loud ocean roar predict a tsunami.
When there is, or has been, a recent tsunami, stay out of the water and away from beaches and waterways
If you are in a tsunami zone and get an official warning, get away from water and climb, the higher the better.
If you are in a tsunami hazard zone and see or hear a natural warning, a tsunami could arrive in minutes.
If officials ask you to evacuate, move quickly to a safe place. Take action immediately. Do not wait for a

more informative official warning, information, or instructions from officials.

Know your community's warning systems and disaster plans, including evacuation routes.

If there is damage, avoid fallen power lines, don't get near any tree (the root structure may be damaged), and stay away from weakened structures.

Get more information about what is happening and what to expect but avoid acting on rumors.

A tsunami watch means the danger level is unknown and you should stay alert for more information.

A tsunami advisory means strong currents are likely and you should stay away from the shore.

A tsunami warning means evacuate because an inundating wave is possible. In a regional tsunami, you may have a few hours to get to safety but if it hits locally, you may only have only 15-20 minutes.

Talk to everyone in your household about what to. Create and practice an evacuation plan. Familiarity may save your life. Be able to follow your escape route at night and during poor weather. You should be able to reach your safe location on foot within 15 minutes. Practicing your plan makes the response more of a reaction, requiring less thinking and reducing panic.

Know the height of your street above sea level and the distance of your street from high tsunami risk areas. Evacuation orders may refer to these numbers.

If you are a tourist at a seaside location, familiarize yourself with local tsunami evacuation protocols. Tourists should always check to see if they are in a tsunami zone.

It is a good idea to pack a flashlight and a dust mask.

Help neighbors who may need special assistance.
Plan evacuation routes for your house, school, workplace, or other areas you frequent. Look for routes that rise 100 feet above sea level or are two miles inland.
Schools are supposed to have evacuation plans in place. Find out what applies to your children.
Have a family reunification plan.
Keep a tsunami evacuation kit by the front door.

If many people evacuate to the same area the local electricity distribution system may not handle the load and fail after initially working. A prudent option is having a generator at the site where you plan to go. Take advantage of local electrical power as long as it is available. Don't forget to store fuel (with added stabilizer and in a controlled location) subject to safety concerns and local regulations.

Your best defense against the effects of this type of event is to stock up on survival food, water, and medical supplies. Because the aftermath is similar to a seismic event, with the addition of mud and silt, the same supplies apply (with the addition of scoop shovels and squeegee floor cleaners). It is crucial to monitor your TV and radio for information as to event scope, duration, or expectations.

In addition to basic supplies listed earlier, store a supply of plastic trash bags and dust masks with breathing valves. Clean off walking areas inside your home while the mud is still liquid. Once it hardens, walking on it will create dust with harmful chemicals. Store temporary toilets, blankets, and extra cash (banks and ATMs will not work).

A tsunami, or any flooding event, problem is that water overwhelms chemical control systems. Waste treatment and industrial chemicals mix into the toxic soup. When this toxic soup contacts your skin, you experience anything from allergic reaction to getting sick. Contact with a dried film of the chemicals on objects you touch can trigger problems too. When it is on the ground, foot traffic results in it a dust.

Water spreads the contamination. The effects of touching contaminated surfaces or breathing (air contains the chemicals) are long-term. You could develop respiratory issues much later. Only go into the area when you wear something like a Tyvek jumpsuit, rubber gloves, shoe covers, hat, and a dust mask. Remember that chemicals often cling to dust particles. Treat it like a pandemic.

It bears repeating. A big assumption is that law enforcement and other emergency services will be available. If even available, they will be overwhelmed and will answer calls for assistance on a lagged basis. If your home is in a tsunami flood zone, store the supplies where you will go and bring them back later.

8   CME or EMP

The main difference between a CME and an EMP event is advance warning. There will probably be no warning of an EMP event. An EMP event damages the power grid and electronics. A CME event affects mostly the power grid, leaving electronics untouched.

There are warning systems between the sun and Earth. They could give us up to a 15-minute warning of a CME event. There is no warning system for an EMP event. Terrorists or a nation-state can detonate a nuclear device that generates an EMP event.

An EMP event has three components (E1, E2, and E3):

The E1 component is very fast and causes a high voltage pulse. It is short but intense and the first effect to arrive. Surge suppressors will not stop this pulse. It creates voltages in wiring and destroys electronics.

The E2 component is like lightning and is easier to eliminate. If the E1 component damages an E2 protection device then the E2 component will cause more damage.

The E3 component is a long pulse. It causes high voltage in long lengths of wire and that shuts down the power grid.

Because EMP travels fast, it is not possible to give a useful warning. Be aware that it is possible that there will be no warning for either a CME or an EMP event. Your best course of action is to plan for no warning and keep spares of critical electronics in an EMP shielded container.

A functioning society depends on electronics (like computers and communications systems). Expect a total breakdown of services and machines, even cars that depend on computer-controlled engines. It would be horrific to experience a CME or EMP event. Daily life would come to a standstill. There would be no control of transportation systems. Delivery trucks would stop. Planes could literally fall out of the sky.

A CME occurs when the solar corona releases plasma that has a magnetic field. When it reaches Earth, the traveling mass causes a geomagnetic storm. The electrical currents it causes are short-lived but strong enough to breakdown or jump insulators. Delicate electronics are especially susceptible to strong CMEs because they can easily overpower them.

These currents quickly dissipate through earth grounds. Because they are short-lived, they reduce to extinction quickly. Unfortunately, this brief time is long enough for them to destroy exposed electronics. One estimate predicts that Earth has a 12% chance of experiencing a strong CME.

What can you do?

The only way to prevent electronics destruction by EMP or CME is to use an electromagnetic shield, i.e., a Faraday cage. You can also protect electronics by burying them under at least three feet of dirt. The dirt blocks magnetic field disturbance. Wait at least an hour to be sure that the CME or EMP event is over.

Grounding a Faraday cage is not required Grounding allows charge to dissipate more quickly. Charge will dissipate anyway because of resistive properties.

Shielding decreases effects of EMP/CME events. It blocks their electromagnetic fields and contains the surface currents they create. A type of shielding is a Faraday cage. It uses an outer layer made of conductive or magnetic material and inner layer of an insulating material. A Faraday cage isolates electrical devices from the outside world.

A Faraday cage distributes an EMP or CME charge around the cage exterior. A Faraday cage is a hollow conductor. No charge is inside the conductor, shielding the interior from exterior charges. Use any metallic conductor to make one. Use an insulating material inside the cage, e.g., cardboard.

For EMP and CME protection, put equipment in boxes in an aluminum trashcan with a tight-fitting lid.

Alternatively, you can wrap a box with heavy-duty aluminum foil.

Aluminum foil tears easily. Protect the wrapped box. If there is a small tear in the aluminum foil, the box no longer works as a Faraday cage.

The effectiveness of Faraday shielding varies depending on construction. Variations in the conductivity of different metals, such as copper or aluminum, affect the cage's function. You can even use enclosing screen if you want to. The size of holes in an enclosing screen or mesh changes its effectiveness.

The effectiveness of Faraday shielding varies on construction. Variations in the conductivity of different metals, such as copper or aluminum, affect the cage's function. You can even use enclosing screen if you want to. The size of holes in an enclosing screen or mesh changes its effectiveness.

An EMP or CME event will cause many effects, from fuel and food shortages to rioting. The first problem will be gathering and transporting fuel, water, medical supplies, and food. Functioning transportation systems will exist if the CME/EMP event affects a limited geographic area. There will be little infrastructure damage, other than electronic controls.

A big initial problem will be malfunctioning traffic control systems. Very few are automated, they require human decision making. Marine, air, and road traffic will halt. Human controllers will resort to manual systems. Vehicles will probably be unaffected because metal shields their electronics but the problem is that when they stop they jam roads.

> Vehicles may lock up. Disconnect and reconnect the
> battery to reboot them. Then start the vehicle.

Functioning transportation systems will move supplies
into a CME/EMP event area. There will be chaotic
supplies distribution. There is a study on the impact of
a CME/EMP event. Its conclusion is that you should
expect one to two years without power. Although the
study used the United States, which has robust
infrastructure, the conclusions apply to any country.

The electrical grid will probably be down, depending
on CME/EMP event strength. The strength of each
diminishes rapidly with distance but if there is more
than one their combined effect is much greater. Have
a PV system or generator available. Extra fuel will run
your generator and car. Extra fuel for your car will
allow you to leave the area.

Your best defense against the effects of this type of
event is to stock up on survival food, water, and
medical supplies, greatly in excess of basic supplies.
People will riot because they are scared. Riots and
survival without external assistance may force you to
isolate yourself. It may take a long time for electrical
power to work again.

Supplies that give you ability to remain out-of-sight
will be invaluable. Limit traveling because you don't
want to encounter a riot. It is crucial to monitor your
TV and radio for information as to riot scope, duration,
changes, or expectations. Riots usually do not have a
leader to direct their actions, expect random behavior.

Use heavy-duty aluminum foil to wrap critical boxed
electronics, making small Faraday cages. You cannot
be certain of event duration so don't take equipment

out of protective Faraday cages too quickly. Faraday cages don't wear out. It is reasonable to expect that sun coronal activity may cause multiple CME events.

A CME event will be short. A strong CME event could have EMP-like effects. If the CME event is strong, aftermath effects will last a long time. It takes a long time to replace damaged electrical grid equipment. Expect at least a one- or two- year delay before infrastructure repairs restore some level of normalcy. In that period, you will need extra stored food and medical supplies.

Based on CME/EMP strength, law enforcement authorities and emergency services may be overwhelmed. Be prepared to provide for your own medical, self-defense, firefighting, and survival needs. Law enforcement will be one of the first services restored, and they will often catch-up on infractions committed during the event.

Expect rioting and looting. People will be scared with a lack of electricity and the problems it causes. The way that people react will be life threatening, to them and to you. Some will take advantage of opportunity to steal. Be prepared to defend what you want to keep but let the rest go. It is not worth being injured or killed. Implement the self-defense actions reviewed in Chapter 3, scaled for event intensity (in other words, focus your actions as warranted by the situation).

9   Rioting

According to Wikipedia, a riot is a form of civil disorder characterized by a group protesting authority. Riots are an irrational reaction to a grievance, dissent, or frustration with the legal system or authorities. Individuals may attempt to lead or control a riot but riots consist of disorganized groups that are chaotic but act with group behavior.

Because a riot is a mass of people acting irrationally, your best defense is to make yourself a lesser target. A riot typically shifts target selection randomly, to focus on more appealing targets. You become a lesser target by looking like you have nothing of interest to the mob. You can also be a lesser target by making your location too difficult for a mob to access (they will move on to the next target).

In general, a riot does not target only you but if one does, it is an attack. Looters often use a riot as cover to either attack or steal; stay vigilant. Riots are usually time-limited but if the cause is unresolved, they can renew and start again. Try to remove yourself from contact with one or take measures to divert it.

What can you do?

Your best defense against this event is to stay unnoticed by not looking like a target that can provide anything the riot wants or appear as though the riot has already visited you. Do not try to appease a mob because that tells it where you are. If you decide to use an active defense, remember a mob has numbers on its side and it does not sleep.

If the riot is local or regional, you can expect external law enforcement activity to help control the situation. If the riot spreads over a larger area then you need to be ready for martial law and curfews until, until it burns-out. As in many of the events listed in this chapter, a riot may breakout when people are frustrated with the level of confusion and chaos resulting from an event.

Your main objective should be to get a mob to go elsewhere. Well-placed animal remains will cause a mob to pause and rethink the need to attack you. Have battery driven motion lights to discourage night attacks (most mob attacks are at night). Use trip wires attached to noisemakers. Remember, this is an all or nothing situation; trying to appease a mob with a partial victory will probably convince it to keep trying.

> If you decide to use non-lethal crowd control, use #6 or #7½ birdshot in a pistol grip, 20-gauge shotgun. Pistol grip shotguns are easier to swing to a new position because they are short. Use a 20-gauge shotgun because it has less recoil (a smaller person may need to use it) compared to a 12-gauge shotgun.

Preparations focus on supplies that help you stay inside your home so you stay hidden and do not call attention to yourself. Remember that any riot, even the self-renewing kind; does not last so long that you need to prepare for a long period of hiding. It is crucial to monitor your radio for information as to riot scope, duration and changes or expectations. Wait at least 24 hours after a riot before leaving your bug-in.

Depending on how long a riot affects you there are a limited number of options to reduce its impact. At first a generator will not be necessary but having it available is useful. We base much of our lives on using electricity so if a riot disrupts availability you will need a secondary source. Minimize its use because the noise it makes attracts attention.

Riot disruptions will limit access to fuel; food; medical and dental facilities; trash pickup; water and sewage utilities; traffic control; and police, fire, and paramedic services. A riot can affect aid distribution and damage infrastructure needed to distribute aid. Depending on how widespread riots are, they could hinder the collection of supplies.

If distribution of supplies is sporadic then assume that utilities will also be sporadic. Electricity will be a big problem because it takes multiple operator coordination to keep a grid-tied system balanced. The best action to take is to store fuel, as limited by your insurance, safety concerns, and local regulations. Having fuel will allow you to run a generator and to run your car so you can get to safety.

Two hallmarks of a rioting event are violence and fires. Because they often happen randomly, assume you must cope with them. In addition to the basic supplies listed at the beginning of this chapter, store facemasks and goggles (to limit smoke inhalation and tear gas effects), a chemical toilet (with enough supplies), and fire extinguishers.

10 Asteroid Impact

Asteroid impact happens when a mass enters the Earth's atmosphere and heat generated by air friction does not consume the mass. There are asteroids that airburst, due to their composition, and shower the target area with fragments. Event effects can range from the extinction of life, to creating small impact craters and dust clouds, to creating a tsunami.

There is a difference between meteors, meteorites, and asteroids but in this book, all forms of objects that hit Earth are asteroids. To be precise, meteorites are objects that hit the planet and asteroids are rocky masses in space (that originate most meteorites). Meteors burn up in the atmosphere.

Luckily, the larger the asteroid is the more likely that we will detect it early. If detected soon enough, NASA should be able to give us warning of when and where it will hit.

Because 70% of Earth's surface is water, it is probable an impact will be in water. At minimum, the heat of the asteroid will flash boil tons of seawater. If the asteroid is large enough its speed could carry it to the ocean floor where it would throw debris into the air.

An ocean impact effect ranges from a tsunami to putting enough flash boiled seawater and particulates into the air to change weather. A land impact would affect close areas. It would put enough particulate matter into the atmosphere to change weather patterns, for years.

All of that matter changes weather patterns in a way that blocks sunlight. Growing seasons will shorten and temperatures will drop. With shortened growing seasons, there will be less food for the planet's population. You should expect rapidly rising prices, shortages, and riots. Food distribution will decrease due to damaged infrastructure.

What can you do?

Reduced nutrition will mean less output of all commodities, which will reduce output even more. The end game for you is to wait for food shortage effects to stabilize. While it is stabilizing, use stored food to avoid exposure to a mob. Availability of food will slowly improve. When it does take advantage of its availability and eat less stored food. Assess event severity and store food accordingly.

As the situation extends, in addition to commodity shortages expect utilities and services to become unreliable. Most services would be available for a "response fee." Responders will need the extra income to cope with increasing food and utility prices because taxes will not rise fast enough to cover their salaries. Use stored cash to pay bribes and response fees.

Authorities will attempt to maintain order as they organize water, food, fuel, and utilities operation. If a riot disrupts electrical utilities, you will need a secondary source of electricity. A large asteroid impact will cause riots when water, food, and fuel distribution disrupts. Expect martial law in any area disrupted by the effects of an asteroid impact.

Your best defense against the effects of this type of event is to stock up on survival food, water, and medical supplies. Riots, thirst, and hunger will be the most probable dangers. Supplies that give you ability to remain out-of-sight of a riot mob will be invaluable. Self-defense against attack or vandalism by mob will be necessary. Be ready to act in self-defense.

Have non-fatal crowd control available, e.g., birdshot or rubber pellets in a pistol grip shotgun. Birdshot will cause pain at 30 yards and bleeding at 10 yards but it is lethal at four yards. Use the shotgun judiciously because any active police will arrest you if you use it inappropriately (as they see it). Police take a dim view of citizens using deadly force.

A major effect will be dust, from impact dust in the air and on the ground In addition to the basic supplies listed earlier store, facemasks and goggles, chemical toilets, fire extinguishers, and extra cash. Consider storing gas masks and extra canisters because they make a better face seal.

> All you need is particulate filtering. Old gas mask
> filter cartridges will do the job.

If there is a long aftermath with minimal agriculture, storing extra food and water will be necessary. Expect that limited amounts of fuel, food, and water will cause hunger and starvation. Growing your own food is labor intensive and requires knowledge of gardening techniques to be successful. Practice gardening on a limited scale, while you can.

During event aftermath, limit traveling away from home because not only do you not want to encounter a riot but also because you do not want to lead anyone back to your supplies. It is crucial to monitor your TV and radio for information as to riot scope, duration, changes, or expectations.

11 Nuclear, Biological, Chemical, or EMP Attack

Nuclear, biological, chemical, or EMP attack would have effects like other survival events but more devastating. Just like an EMP, nation-states could supply a terrorist organization with a weapon and direct its use, giving the nation-state deniability. The purpose of any attack is to cause as much damage, confusion, and fear as possible.

Review the recommended preparations for any survival event, especially pandemics; they have similar effects. Besides being artificial events, they also have a common purpose to disrupt services. Services support a functioning infrastructure. Disrupting them will make any response difficult.

Biological attacks have effects much like a pandemic. Nuclear attacks have effects much like a seismic event (see event 7) coupled with an asteroid impact (see event 10) but include radiation effects. An EMP attack would have effects much like a CME event.

There are two types of nuclear attack: dirty bomb or nuclear explosion. A dirty bomb uses ordinary explosives to disperse radioactive particles. Particle dispersion depends on mostly environmental factors, primarily wind speed and direction. Its purpose is to create fear and confusion. It will kill more people by the explosives blast than by radiation.

A nuclear explosion kills people and destroys infrastructure. If terrorists detonate one, the intention is to create panic. If a nation-state detonates one, they want to stay unknown or end a war before retribution.

Nuclear explosion ionizing radiation disrupts cells within an organism. There are many types of ionizing radiation but the most common are alpha, beta and gamma radiation. Thick layers of dense materials stop ionizing radiation. Any material stops ionizing radiation if it is thick enough.

The physical effects of a dirty bomb or a nuclear detonation are different. The shockwave of a nuclear explosion creates physical damage. It shatters windows and creates flying glass. You can filter radioactive particles from a dirty bomb out of the air, or clean them up if they are surface dust.

The explosion of a nuclear bomb has EMP effects. If it detonates at a high enough altitude, the blast effects will be limited. Distance, explosion magnitude, and shielding determine the strength of EMP effects. EMP effects do not harm people but they can destroy electronics.

What can you do?

In case of a nuclear attack, follow the steps listed here for CME/EMP or pandemic events. A CME/EMP event will be similar and a biological attack will be similar to a pandemic. In case of a nuclear attack, limit radiation exposure by staying indoors and underground as fallout decreases but remember that what you can't see can still hurt or kill you.

Potassium iodate (KIO3) often is thought of as a safeguard against all radiation effects—**it is not**. KIO3 only protects the thyroid gland from accumulation of radioactive iodine compounds.

Thyroid gland disruption by radioactive iodine compounds causes a lingering death. Dirty bombs disperse radioactive iodine compounds. KIO3 could be useful to have because terrorists could detonate a dirty bomb. **The FDA has not approved KIO3 for blocking radioactive iodine**.

A chemical attack can be either small or large scale. Although the wind will disperse most of it, heavier than air pockets may remain. Stay in your shelter until you hear an all-clear message. Your shelter probably has enough air but if not, breathe only filtered air.

Chemical attacks can cause a wide variety of effects. These effects are created to keep you confused, panicked, and uncertain of what to do and in doing so spread fear among the general population. The biggest danger is to act without considering unintended consequences, or to be part of a mob that causes acts for which you are accountable.

The first problems will be gathering and transporting fuel, water, and food. Be prepared for unreliable access to food, water, and fuel and for limitations due to contamination. If an attack event happens, expect follow-up attacks as other countries attempt to take advantage of panic and confusion.

Your best defense against chemical attacks is to store survival food, water, and medical supplies. Depending on intensity of an attack, there will be infrastructure disruptions. Disruptions will limit delivery of food, fuel, and medicine. Panic and fear will increase the effects of disruptions and shortages.

Limit traveling away from home because not only do you not want to encounter a riot but also you do not want to lead anyone back to your supplies. It is crucial to monitor your TV and radio for information as to scope, duration, changes, or expectations for the event.

Store a supply of facemasks, and goggles (to limit exposure to or inhalation of radioactive dust), plastic trash bags, basic medical supplies, temporary toilets, fire extinguishers, and extra cash. Cash because banks and ATMs will not work (but don't advertise it exists).

You need to be ready to act in your own self-defense because other survivors will try to take your supplies. Distribution of new supplies will be chaotic and disorderly. Have some form of non-fatal self-defense available. Defend against an advancing mass of people intent on overpowering you and taking your supplies.

12 Super-Volcano, Black Hole, or Gamma Ray Burst

Massive super-volcano/black hole/gamma ray burst events have effects that exceed reasonable precautions but have an extremely low probability of occurring, but not zero. If the event is cosmological (resulting from uncontrollable events in outer space) then the extreme magnitude of this type of event will cause problems beyond our ability to foresee.

Stephen Hawking, the late brilliant British cosmologist, advocated that the human species populate other celestial bodies. His belief was that this was the only way to avoid the extreme effects of a cosmological event hitting Earth.

Terrestrial events, like the eruption of a super-volcano, although potentially massive, are survivable. The human race will have to change to survive in the new environment.

What can you do?
This type of event is a The End of The World as We Know It (TEOTWAWKI) event. It may not be survivable. Life after a TOTAWAKI event will be extremely difficult to cope with. Intensity of the event will determine its final survival impact.

Some of the events in this class may occur as less intense events. For instance, there is a theory that extraordinarily small black holes pass through the planet frequently, causing odd weather and seismic events. Another possibility is that a major seismic event (like a super-volcano) might happen at a lesser intensity.

Notes: Likely Events

Notes: Likely Events

Chapter 10
Bug-in or Bug-out?

Although you should bug-in for most survival events, there are times when it will be prudent to bug-out. You can make a response between bug-in and bug-out. It is an extended bug-in. An extended bug-in is like backyard camping. Consider an extended bug-in before deciding to bug-out.

You should gather information to help you decide whether (and when) to extend your bug-in, or whether to proceed directly to bugging-out. It is reckless to take any action without evaluating whether the situation is stable or changing. An estimate of the relative probabilities for an event occurring during normal life is:

L1	50%	Bug-in*
L2	15%	Bug-in*
L3	4%	Extended bug-in*
L4	.001%	Bug-out**
L5	.0000000001%	Bug-out**

* If bugging-in is impossible, bug-out.
** Decide if the event has stabilized and where it is safe.

Maintain a "can and will do" attitude about dealing with the aftermath of any survival event. Feeling sorry for yourself and despairing about what happened (and is happening) leads to poor daily performance and ineffective task completion. Poorly performed tasks often have dire or fatal consequences. A major problem is that a seemingly meaningless result can have big implications for follow-up tasks.

Infrastructure damage will be the biggest factor determining how long you need to survive. It will limit your movement and access to external aid. Infrastructure damage repairs will take time but you have access to stored supplies and have detailed knowledge of the surrounding area. Use repair time to your advantage by adding to your supplies. Repairs may not work out as planned.

Bug-in

Bugging-in is usually the best first approach. It is valid to bug-in first and later decide to bug-out. Bugging-in without preparing can get you killed, just as easily as easily as bugging-out can. It is reckless to take action without knowing if the situation is stable.

If the event is stable, bug-in as long as possible before deciding to transition to a bug-out. Usually the only way to tell if an event is stable is to wait to see if the main event continues or related damage makes survival difficult. If events make it impossible to survive by bugging-in, immediately bug-out.

When you bug-in you don't want to deal with survivors who will be preying on other survivors. Staying bugged-in can attract looters. Looters prefer to prey on someone else rather than risk his/her life if you are resisting.

On the other hand, if you look well supplied a looter may consider you a target worth the risk. Try to remain unnoticed and leave your bug-in home as little as possible, using your stored supplies to stay isolated. Remember that bugging-in when an event changes makes you standout.

Realize that events may take time to stabilize. Do not take excessive time trying to determine if what you know is fully accurate. As George Patton said, acting in the next 5 minutes on uncertain information is often better than waiting 10 minutes to act on certain information.

He also said, "If everybody is thinking alike, somebody isn't thinking." Take this to mean you need to determine for yourself what an event could become. Act accordingly, not just following what everyone else is doing. Deciding to bug-out is a decision with irreversible consequences.

Extended Bug-in

There is an intermediate step between a bug-in and a bug-out; an extended bug-in. An extended bug-in is like camping in your backyard, or nearby, where you still have full access to your supplies. If your home has sustained structural damage, you may be able to make repairs and get access to stored supplies.

It is prudent to have basic supplies hidden near your home, like burying them in a waterproof container or using an out building. Have enough remote supplies to meet initial needs and give you time to retrieve your main supplies.

An extended bug-in does not replace a bug-out. Assess the event situation. If there is a good chance that external aid will arrive then do not bug-out, unless the situation where you are becomes untenable or life threatening.

Bug-out

Bug-out is an overused term because people don't understand the implications. If you bug-out too quickly, you risk not gathering information about event changes that could affect your decision. Bugging-out has inherent dangers, more than bugging-in.

"Experts" often tout bugging-out and using wilderness skills as the best solution for every survival situation. Planning to use wilderness skills is glamorous but not practical. The same experts often charge to learn wilderness skills in classes they offer.

Bugging-out is not as simple as it appears. It is likely that roads will clog with people trying to bug-out. Road system design is for typical daily use, not for an overwhelming volume of traffic.

Don't try to bug-out unless you know you will be one of the first and that there are no population centers between you and your destination. You are much better off waiting and gathering information, before deciding to leave your known bug-in for an unknown bug-out.

Waiting will be mentally difficult and it could last as long as a month, or more. What you are waiting for is for the event to stabilize, for infrastructure repairs to make aid possible, and for survivor violence to minimize.

If you do decide to bug-out, be prepared for violent encounters. Travel as far as you can by car but, inevitably, there will be traffic jams or damaged roads and bridges. Be prepared to load your supplies on a cart (that you brought) and walk, pushing the cart or riding a bicycle that is towing the cart.

If the event is stable at L2, bug-in as long as possible with a low probability of needing to bug-out. If the event is stable at L3 or L4, then bug-in as long as possible with a need to understand if the event will stay stable. Consider the probability that it will become unstable. You may need to bug-out immediately if the event is unstable.

In L4/L5 survival events, consider the effects of a supportive group of other survivors. Effects of an L4/L5 event will be long lasting and will redefine life styles. Hearing the thoughts of others may save you from pursuing bad ideas. Refer to Chapter 8 for more detail on self-sufficiency.

If the event appears stable at L4, then bug-in at first and plan to bug-out when bugging-in is no longer realistic. If the event is stable at L5, plan to bug-out immediately. Assess your survival chances where you are and consider where you might go to survive safely. If you bug-out plan to join a group of other survivors so you can share resources and skills.

What can you do?

You should have a written plan; with options for event variations. Give copies to all members of your survival group and practice what each person needs to be able to do. Practice makes actions automatic and when an event happens, there will be less confusion and stress. Purchase whatever supplies the plan refers to and be sure that all survival group members know where the supplies are and how to use them.

Go over specific responsibilities in the plan, as a group. Each person needs to have group reinforcement of individual responsibilities. Knowing that others are depending on him/her will motivate the responsible person. Take time to work with the individual to find out what is difficult for them to understand or do. You don't want them to have problems with it later.

Knowing that others depend on them makes individuals see themselves as part of a group. Knowing that you belong to a group is a strong motivator. This reinforces group loyalty and that results in strong bonds with group members. This feedback loop builds teamwork and dependable mutual support.

Having an organized plan is a good start. Expect the unexpected by making a plan as flexible as possible. Changes can hinder using a plan effectively. The worst case is when one or more group members don't gather after an event. Cross training group members helps to overcome the no-show problem. Cross training has other benefits, e.g., backup in case of injury or illness, a second opinion, and teamwork.

Practice is key because there will be no time for training after an event happens. Every adult group member should have immediate access to an EDC kit and a GHB. Make plans with children and the elderly so they know what to expect from you and what you are depending on them to do. The main point is that knowing what to do will distract them from panic.

- **EDC**

    Do not tell others that it exists or about its contents. If it is visible and someone asks, say it contains items for your personal needs. Do **not** keep a firearm in it because it will be accessible by others. Below are suggested contents for an EDC kit (small enough to fit in a waist pack) that you keep with you, to help you to get home or to your GHB:

    - about 8 feet of parachute cord
    - lightweight emergency poncho (with hood)
    - printed topographic waterproof map of the area
    - N95/N100 dust mask
    - cell phone, charger, cable
    - wallet with ID and keys
    - space blanket
    - multi-tool with screwdrivers, pliers, and saw
    - adjustable flashlight
    - disposable butane lighter
    - P51 can opener
    - folding knife, 3.5-inch blade, lock-back
    - small first aid kit

- **GHB**

    A GHB (small enough for a sling pack, in addition to EDC kit) is a more comprehensive EDC kit. Keep your GHB in your possession; it may have a firearm in it. Realize that if it contains a firearm that you may need to leave it behind because some places prohibit it (like courts or airports).

    A good rule of thumb is always having your EDC kit with you. Its purpose is to help you get to your bug-in. If you travel more than 30 miles from home bring your GHB too.

    - 10 feet (more) of parachute cord
    - emergency food
    - 4, ½-liter containers of water, refillable
    - water disinfectant
    - pea-less whistle
    - headlamp with spare batteries
    - 2 blankets, 1 wool and 1 more space blanket
    - windproof matches and another disposable lighter
    - tinder to make a fire (like dryer lint)
    - shoes suitable for walking
    - warm hat, socks, underwear, and jacket
    - gloves
    - spare batteries for the EDC flashlight
    - heavier poncho (with hood)
    - 3 sealable one-gallon freezer baggies
    - another N95/N100 dust mask
    - toilet paper and hand sanitizer
    - augmented first aid kit
    - flashlight with batteries and spare batteries
    - sunglasses
    - sunscreen
    - compass (lensatic for versatility but a simple one is OK)
    - digging device (trowel or folding shovel)

- AM/FM/weather radio, portable, extra batteries
- another P51 can opener
- duct tape, at least 20 feet

- **BOB**

  The first and best option is to bug-in but some events require an immediate bug-out. Having and using a BOB is a last resort for when the situation changes. A BOB gives you ability to take supplies with you if forced to leave a bug-in. Consider conditions around your destination before you leave.

  Have a pre-packed BOB where you can get to it, quickly. You will not have time to scurry around collecting items. Resist the temptation to use BOB supplies in your bug-in.

  Use a BOB to collect items but plan to move it using a cart to manage the weight (walking is much easier and using it leaves your hands free). As heavy as it is, it holds items that will sustain a person for less than two weeks. This is a suggested BOB list of supplies; making the BOB too heavy to carry (for most people):

  - pair of walking shoes
  - hat with a 4-inch brim
  - shemagh (head scarf, face mask, filter, sling, sponge, etc.)
  - multi-pocket vest

    This item carries personal survival supplies, wear it at all times. If there is violence that separates you from your supplies, you still have supplies that you carry with you. Do not overload it because the extra weight will make you less nimble and slower trying to get away.

  - 4 empty canteens, 1 and 2 quarts

- empty water bottle wrapped with duct tape
- filtering water bottle with a spare filter
- 2 empty 1-gallon water carriers
- bottle of 2% tincture of iodine
- tubes of (water) flavor enhancer tablets
- emergency drinking straw (in vest)
- weather alert radio-solar, battery, hand-cranked
- emergency survival sleeping bag (in vest)
- 175 feet of paracord
- multi-tool
- packet of emergency cash, $400, small bills
- night glow marker (attached to BOB carry handle)
- knife sharpener
- camp light with spare battery
- 20-watt portable folding solar panel
- Li-ion battery pack
- rechargeable batteries
- 4 bay battery recharging station
- survival knife (Figure 10) (keep it with you)

There are more uses for a dependable survival knife than there is room to list. This particular knife is a kukri type. Its design shifts some blade weight towards the tip. The shifted blade weight is useful for chopping and hacking.

Figure 11 is a picture of the fire starter and sharpening supplies that you keep with the knife.

Note in Figure 12 that this knife is full tang (metal end-to-end) and that there is a hole in the handle for attaching a lanyard.

Figure 13 shows a feature for hammering on things like tent stakes or cracking open hulls.

 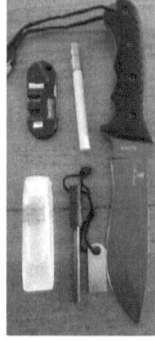  

Figure 10.　　Figure 11.　　Figure 12.　　Figure 13.

- headlamp with spare alkaline batteries
- spiral ring notepad with a Sharpie and a space pen
- N95 dust mask with a breathing valve
- N100 dust mask with a breathing valve
- disposable lighters (high wind and no wind)
- bag of fire-starters (tinder)
- WoundMedic kit, minor wounds
- instant cold pack, single use
- blister kit
- light-duty space blanket, for shelter and medical
- heavy-duty space blanket, personal use (in vest)
- *SAS Survival Handbook*

  This book is indispensable!

- emergency food bars
- sunglasses
- knot tying guide
- emergency poncho, hooded, in vest
- heavy-duty poncho, hooded
- topographical maps, local and state
- compass (lensatic for versatility)
- small bar of soap and small washcloth
- alcohol based hand sanitizer
- insect repellant
- gloves
- windbreaker, hooded

- nylon tarp for simple shelter (nylon is quiet)

  A simple shelter is something you can erect quickly, no matter where you are. Weather, location, and available materials determine what configuration you use. This is a picture of only one alternative configuration. Learn more than one so you have options.

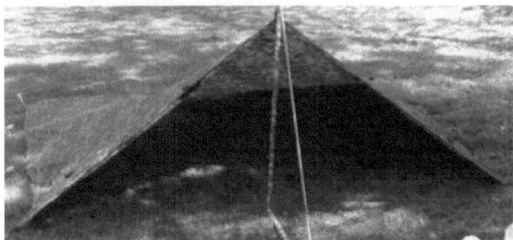

Figure 14. Simple shelter

- tarp tie-down clamps
- light and heavy-duty stakes
- tent front pole (there may not be anything to use)
- waist pack with basic clothing
- extra socks (damp socks breed debilitating disease)
- water resistant rucksack with cold weather clothing and 2 pair of boots (1 waterproof and 1 for cold weather)
- flash drive with scans of all important documents for each group member. Use an encrypted, waterproof, EMP/CME proof case:

Active Rx's	drivers license(s)	marriage license	Medicare card	life insurance
credit cards	concealed carry permit(s)	passport	medical insurance	dental insurance
mortgage	military ID	will and DNR	car registration and insurance	prescription insurance
loans	birth certificate	social security card	home/rental insurance	medical records
blood type	disabilities documents	dental records	allergy information	pet records
family photos to help find someone	property title(s)	supplies inventory	recent bank statement(s)	fishing and hunting licenses

If you have prescription medications, have extra, but watch the expiration date. If you are caring for a baby, children, the elderly, or the disabled you need their supplies and medications too. Caring for children and the elderly needs to account for short attention spans and inconsistent memory, which means needing to keep them occupied.

Using a BOB typically means that you have no time to waste trying to find items. Keep your BOB packed and ready. It should be stored where you can quickly retrieve it. Don't display it or tell others where it is, or that it even exists. If children are involved, be judicious about letting them know that BOBs exist. They will want to show it to friends, who will talk. It is not a play toy; make sure they understand that.

If there is time to prepare for a bug-out you can add a pre-packed Bug Out Pack (BOP) but do not plan on carrying it.

- **BOP**

  A BOP is even heavier than a BOB but provides equipment to sustain you indefinitely, assuming you forage and scavenge too. A BOP is an addition to your BOB. A BOP has limited food and no water but it has water-filtering equipment:

  - sealed clothing bag
  - three-man tent
  - open mesh ground tarp for tent
  - one-man anti-bug summer sleeping bivvy
  - monocular, for distance viewing
  - 250 feet more of paracord
  - 2.5-gallon collapsible water carrier
  - hanging pouch water filter

- metal water bottle
- gravity type filtration system, squeeze type is OK
- bottle of Polar Pure iodine
- comprehensive first aid kit
- nested cooking stove and pot
- nested cooking kit
- folding metal trowel
- fire grate
- refillable butane lighter/pocket torch
- can of butane fuel to refill lighters
- tube of firestarter paste
- magnesium fire-starter
- solid fuel, trioxane tablets, do not breathe vapors
- packs of butane lighters
- storm-proof matches
- extra long matches
- adjustable flame butane lighters
- strike anywhere matches
- tinder fire straws
- thumb hole plastic plates
- spork (fork, knife, and spoon eating utensil)
- plastic cup
- camouflage duct tape
- knife sharpener
- multi-tool
- Swiss army-type knife, for a general-purpose camp tool
- compact firearm cleaning kit (all calibers rifle or pistol)
- hygiene bag:
  - 3 bars of soap
  - 1 oz and 1.5 oz hand sanitizer
  - 8.2 oz toothpaste
  - 4 oz waterless/dry shampoo
  - 90 flossers
  - toothbrush

- 4 oz camp suds, concentrated
- fingernail clippers

- **Sleep System**

    A necessary addition is a sleep system. It is a system because when correctly used it is a set of three sleeping bags (with an optional liner) that acts like layered clothes. A full sleeping system is a washable inner liner, a lightweight summer sleeping bag or blanket, a cold weather sleeping bag and a bivvy cover.

    It is too bulky to pack in a BOP. It is possible to put together a sleep system from ad-hoc materials. Using ad-hoc materials may result in painful consequences. Leave this route to practiced outdoorsmen (and women). A goodnight's sleep enhances your ability to make good decisions. When you need to survive, every decision may be critical.

    You will face a long list of decisions to make and tasks to perform. Lack of restful sleep will cloud your judgment and cause accidents. Just the anxiety of the situation and stress of day-to-day survival will reduce restful sleep. It may be useful to use a non-habit forming sleep-aid.

    Insects, vermin, snakes, and other animals are nighttime pests. Your body heat attracts them. Event aftermath will stress them too. Expect bolder activity from them to intrude on your life. To keep insects and other pests from disturbing your sleep, use a bivvy sleeping bag cover with a mosquito net over your head. You will need to use something to hold the net away from your face.

A bivvy cover is waterproof and bug-proof. Depending on what you get, it may even be resistant to animal bites. You can use the bivvy cover by itself (e.g., in the summer to repel mosquitoes) or with other parts of the system when you need to sleep outdoors.

This page intentionally blank.

Notes: Bug-in or Bug-out?

Notes: Bug-in or Bug-out?

Chapter 11
Now What?

There are many types of survival events. This book uses relative probabilities to prioritize bug-in preparations. Expectations for what might happen where you live define preparations. There are basic bug-in preparations, see Chapter 9, common to all survival events.

The single biggest survival event is unfolding. As severe weather continues to intensify into extreme weather, there are conflicting and confusing reasons offered. People usually ignore conflicting or confusing data and believe conditions are a new normal.

The problem is that any new normal will not be constant. Episodes of extreme weather cause a need for you to be able to react immediately. Immediate survival may become difficult but surviving in the aftermath could create conditions that stretch outside aid to the breaking point. Expect to depend on yourself.

An example is that since warmer air holds more water, there has been extraordinary rain and snow, leading to widespread flooding. Flooding often causes crop failures. Crop failures lead to food shortages. Food shortages can cause interruptions of fuel deliveries and services. Interruptions often cause riots and aggressive behavior.

Stand back and you get a glimpse of how reaction to a survival event will unfold. Effects from this pandemic are slow moving and containable. Another pandemic might be faster and more virulent. Such a pandemic would be far less containable. You are seeing many types of event collateral effects for the first time. These effects are common to all possible survival events. They are relatively mild to this point, **but it may not stay that way**.

Book Two of the *Plan to Survive* series examines more extensive preparations. The basic preparations outlined in Chapter 9 of this book are sufficient for the majority of possible survival events. Book Two helps you enhance your level of preparation. Preparing does not need to be expensive if you plan.

Your opinion matters. It will matter more if people know. Posting an Amazon book review will help others. To post a review go to http://www.amazon.com/review/create-review?&asin=B07Y4LMNSM or create one on the book's Amazon product page review area for *Plan to Survive I*.

Glossary

Definitions of terms refer to how this book uses the term. Wikipedia provided most of the definitions material.

Some of the terms appear in other books of the *Plan to Survive* series but are included here for reference.

absolute micron rating
Absolute micron rating is the diameter of the largest particle that passes through a filter. Another way of thinking of this is that the rating is the size of the largest filter pore.

amino acid
Nine of the 20 standard amino acids are "essential" amino acids. They cannot be synthesized from other compounds by the human body, and must be taken in as food. Others may be essential for some ages or medical conditions.

analog radio signal
An analog radio signal is a method of conveying information using a continuous signal that varies in amplitude, phase, or waveform frequency. It uses an analog method such as frequency modulation (FM) or amplitude modulation (AM). Digital signals are not continuous (analog).

ARRL
The **A**mateur **R**adio **R**elay **L**eague represents the interests of amateur radio operators at regulatory bodies and provides technical advice and assistance.

bacitracin
Bacitracin is an antibiotic used as a topical preparation (as it can cause kidney damage when used internally). It may slow healing in otherwise sterile wounds if used repeatedly.

bivvy bag
> A bivvy bag is like a waterproof jacket for your sleeping bag. It's a thin, waterproof bag. A bivvy bag is less expensive than a tent.

benzalkonium chloride
> Benzalkonium chloride (BZK) is an antiseptic used to disinfect wound areas and hands.

BOB
> A **b**ug **o**ut **b**ag (BOB) supports a bug-out. Use it for surviving with very limited supplies or limited assistance. See GOOD or INCH.

BOL
> A **b**ug **o**ut location (BOL) is a remote bug out destination. Supplies are often stored there.

bolt action
> Bolt action is a type of firearm action where the handling of cartridges into and out of the weapon's barrel chamber is operated by manually manipulating the bolt. Bolt action designs have potential for superior accuracy.

BOP
> A **b**ug **o**ut **p**ack (BOP) is a large pack of survival supplies that augments a BOB. It extends the length of survival time when used with a BOB. It contains no water and limited food.

BPA
> **B**is**p**henol **A** (BPA) is a chemical additive to polycarbonate plastics to make them stiff. BPA is a xenoestrogen, with estrogen-mimicking, hormone-like properties. Since 2008, several governments have investigated its safety, which prompted some retailers to withdraw polycarbonate products.

buck transformer

Also known as a buck boost transformer, it adjusts voltage applied to alternating current equipment. Use buck transformers to regulate the voltage going to delicate or sensitive electronic equipment.

BZK

See *benzalkonium chloride.*

calcium hypochlorite

Calcium hypochlorite is the main active ingredient of commercial products used for water treatment and as a bleaching agent. It is sold as pool shock to treat swimming pools.

catalysis and catalyze

Catalysis is the process of increasing the rate of a chemical reaction by adding a substance known as a catalyst. Catalyzed substances remain when catalysis is complete.

CCD

A **c**harge **c**oupled **d**evice (CCD) uses digital manipulation to duplicate an image on a screen. The process begins with light modifying electrical properties of the device.

choil

A choil is an indentation in the handle or blade of a knife used for control when attempting fine work.

CME

A **c**oronal **m**ass **e**jection is a large release of plasma, with a magnetic field, from the sun.

CMOS

A **c**omplimentary **m**etal **o**xide semiconductor (CMOS) uses digital manipulation to duplicate an image on a screen. The process begins with light modifying electrical properties of the device.

CO (carbon monoxide)
Carbon monoxide (CO) is a colorless, odorless, and tasteless gas that is slightly less dense than air. It is toxic to animals that use hemoglobin as an oxygen carrier.

CO_2 (carbon dioxide)
Carbon dioxide (CO_2) is a colorless gas with a density about 60% higher than dry air. At high concentrations, it has a sharp and acidic odor and a bitter taste.

coagulant
Coagulation, known as clotting, is the process by which blood changes from liquid to gel, helping to form a scab. Coagulation begins almost instantly after an injury.

compression bandage
A compression bandage is one that applies pressure to a wound to stop any bleeding. An injured person can use a compression bandage.

cyber-mischief
Cyber-mischief is activity that involves a computer and a network. Cyber-mischief may threaten a person, company, or a nation's security and financial health. It is an umbrella term that can refer to cybercrime, malware, cyber-attacks, ransomware, etc.

designator
A designator is a laser sight that projects a visible dot of light that designates a target.

desiccant
A desiccant absorbs water vapor (humidity). A desiccant is a substance that causes a state of dryness in its vicinity. Most pre-packaged desiccants absorb water and water vapor.

digital radio signal

Digital radio signals use digital technology to transmit or receive. An analog signal is digitized and compressed then transmitted by using digital techniques.

dirty bomb

A dirty bomb disperses radioactive material by using explosives. The purpose is to contaminate the area around the explosion with radioactive material. It is primarily an area denial device. A dirty bomb is unlikely to cause many deaths by radiation exposure. It creates psychological, not physical, harm through ignorance, panic, and terror.

distillation

Distillation separates substances in a liquid by using selective boiling and condensation. Distillation is the traditional method of desalination and water purification.

dosimeter

A radiation dosimeter is a device that measures the cumulative dose of external ionizing radiation. Modern electronic dosimeters give a continuous readout of cumulative dose and current dose rate.

drone

A drone is an unmanned aerial vehicle (UAV). It is a component of a system composed of: a UAV, a ground-based controller, and a system of communications between the ground and the UAV.

U.S. civilian users must register (other requirements too) any UAV over .55 pounds in weight and license their right to use it.

drop-point knife

A drop point knife is a style of knife blade that curves a tip downward from the spine of the blade. This allows the spine of the blade (where the blade is thicker and stronger) to continue forward to the tip of the blade. This eliminates pitching when stabbing.

EDC

An **every day carry** (EDC) kit is a collection of items carried by a person every day. The main reasons for having an EDC kit are utility and preparedness to help individuals overcome simple problems and to deal with unexpected and dangerous situations.

electrical grid

The electrical grid is an interconnected network for delivering electricity from producers. It uses power stations to produce electrical power, transmission lines to move electricity, and distribution lines to connect to users.

electrolyte

An electrolyte is a substance that produces an electrically conducting solution when dissolved in water. In medicine, electrolyte replacement is needed when a person has prolonged vomiting or diarrhea, and as a response to strenuous athletic activity.

EMP

An **electromagnetic pulse** (EMP) is a short burst of electromagnetic energy. Its origination may be natural or manmade. It can produce a radiated, electric, magnetic field, or a conducted electric current. EMP interference is disruptive or damaging to electronic equipment.

EMP shielding

EMP shielding reduces an electromagnetic field by blocking the field with barriers made of conductive or magnetic materials. Shielding is typically applied to enclosures to isolate electrical devices from their surroundings. EMP Shielding can contain surface currents caused by electromagnetic fields. The amount of reduction on material used, its thickness, the size of the shielded volume and the frequency of electromagnetic fields, shape, and orientation of shield holes. See Faraday cage.

expectorant

An expectorant is part of a chemical agent that aids in the clearance of mucus and particulates from the upper and lower airways. Expectorants treat respiratory diseases caused by inhalation of particulates.

Faraday cage

A Faraday cage or shield is an enclosure used to block electromagnetic fields. A Faraday shield is a continuous covering of conductive material, or in the case of a Faraday cage, by a mesh of material. See EMP shielding.

fast reaction force

A fast reaction force is an armed group that responds quickly to emergency needs.

FEMA

Federal Emergency Management Agency is an agency of the United States Department of Homeland Security. Its primary purpose is to coordinate response to a disaster that overwhelms resources of local and state authorities.

ferrocerium rod

Ferrocerium is a synthetic material that produces sparks when rapidly oxidized. Rapid oxidation comes from the process of striking/scraping it against steel.

fiat money

A currency established as legal tender by government regulation. Fiat money does not have a natural value. It only has value because a government maintains its value, or because parties engaging in exchange agree on its value. It exists as an alternative to commodity money and representative money.

fixed-blade knife

A fixed-blade knife is heavier and stronger than a folding knife. It usually has a full tang (full-length metal). In survival supplies, it is a survival knife and has multiple job uses.

FLIR

Forward-looking infrared (FLIR) systems use a camera that senses infrared radiation. FLIR sensors use detection of infrared radiation from a heat source, to create video image. Infrared wavelengths thermal imaging cameras can detect is 3-12 μm (1 μm is one millionth of a meter). It differs from night vision, which operates in the visible light and near-infrared ranges. FLIR systems can detect concealed objects.

freeze-dried food

Freeze-drying is a low temperature dehydration process that uses freezing the product, lowering pressure, and removing ice by sublimation (converting from a solid directly to a gas). This is in contrast to dehydration by most conventional methods that evaporate water using heat.

FRS

The family radio service is an improved walkie-talkie radio system authorized in the United States since 1996. This radio service uses frequencies 462 MHz and 467 MHz in the UHF band. FRS signals use frequency modulation.

funneling effect
The funneling effect is limiting the freedom of walking movement to a specific path.

gen 1 (NV)
Generation 1 (night vision) increases light using a light amplification tube. See *night vision.*

gen 2 (NV)
Generation 2 (Night Vision) uses a better light amplification tube (see above).

gen 2+ (NV)
Generation 2+ (Night Vision) uses a light sensitive semiconductor to display images.

GHB
A get home bag (GHB) is a collection of items that aid getting from where you are to your home. It is stored because it is too large to keep with you. In comparison, an EDC bag is small enough to keep with you and can get you to your GHB, or home.

ghillie
A ghillie (suit, parka, blanket, or net) is a type of camouflage that resembles the background around it. The purpose is to obscure visibility. It is usually made with loosely woven netting that holds strips of cloth or local foliage

GMRS
A ground mobile radio service (GMRS) is a land-mobile UHF radio service designed for short-distance communication. The United States permits use by adult individuals who possess a GMRS license, as well as immediate family members. It shares some frequencies with FRS radios.

GOOD
A get out of dodge (GOOD) bag is a BOB. See *BOB.*

GPS

The **g**lobal **p**ositioning **s**ystem (GPS) is a satellite-based navigation system owned by the United States government and operated by the United States Space Force. Obstacles such as mountains and buildings block the relatively weak GPS signals.

gravity filtration

Gravity filtration is a method of filtering impurities by using gravity to pull liquid through a filter.

grid down

Grid down refers to when the electrical grid is not working. See electrical grid definition.

HDPE

High-**d**ensity **p**olyethylene (HDPE) is a polymer with high strength-to-density. The production of food packaging uses HDPE. It uses the identification code 2.

HEPA

High **e**fficiency **p**articulate **a**ir (HEPA) is a rating for air filters. HEPA filters must satisfy certain levels of efficiency (in the U.S. it is 99.97% of particles whose diameter is as small as 0.3 μm).

HF radio

High **f**requency (HF) is the designation for frequencies between 3 and 30 megahertz. Higher frequencies are the very high frequency (VHF) band. The HF band is a major part of shortwave frequencies, so communication at these frequencies is shortwave radio. Because the atmosphere reflects these radio waves back to Earth by, these frequencies are suitable for long-distance communication and for mountainous terrains that prevent line-of-sight communications.

honey pot

As used in this book, a honey pot is a trap intended to appear as a place for an attacker to hide or a path to attack a target. Often a honey pot appears to offer obvious access to target vulnerabilities in order to make it tempting for attackers to use.

housekeeping

As used in this book, it means conducting routine tasks to maintain a daily function, e.g. monitoring radio traffic.

HP

Hollow point (HP) ammunition is an expanding bullet used to control penetration. Over-penetration can cause unwanted collateral damage. Impact forces fluid into the bullet nose cavity, causing bullet lead to mushroom outward. Hollow point bullets are more accurate and predictable compared to pointed bullets (FMJ).

hydrocortisone cream

Hydrocortisone cream is the term for cortisol used in topical application. It is an immune system suppressive drug. It is used for allergic rashes, eczema, psoriasis, itching, and other inflammatory skin conditions. Covering the skin increases absorption.

hyperthermia

Hyperthermia, also known as overheating, is a condition where an individual's temperature is elevated due to failed thermoregulation, causing the body to produce or absorb more heat than it dissipates.

hypothermia

Hypothermia is when body core temperature is below 35.0 °C (95.0 °F). In mild hypothermia, there is shivering and mental confusion. In moderate hypothermia, shivering stops and confusion increases. Extreme hypothermia often results in death.

INCH bag

An **I**'m **n**ever **c**oming **h**ome (INCH) bag is a BOB. See *BOB*.

infrared (IR)

Infrared is electromagnetic radiation with longer wavelengths than visible light. Infrared light is invisible to the human eye but the source may be detectable.

inverter

An inverter converts AC voltage and current to DC voltage and current.

IR illuminator

An IR illuminator projects infrared light to increase illumination for NV devices. See NV.

JHP

A **j**acketed **h**ollow-**p**oint (JHP) bullet is a hollow point bullet (see *HP*) in which the bullet is encased in a harder material, to limit bullet expansion on impact.

karambit knife

A karambit knife can be drawn and slash in one movement. It curves and looks like an animal claw.

kydex

Kydex is a thermoplastic acrylic-polyvinyl chloride material manufactured by Sekisui SPI. It has a wide variety of applications, including holsters and knife sheaths.

lidocaine

Lidocaine, also known as lignocaine, is a medication used to numb tissue in a specific area. It is a topical local anesthetic.

light discipline

Light discipline is concealing the observation of light at night. Visible light is an indication of the presence of targets for intrusion.

light emitting diode (LED)
A light emitting diode is a semiconductor material that emits light when current flows through it.

marine VHF radio
Marine VHF radio uses the frequency range 156-174 MHz. Modern marine VHF radios have transmit and receive capabilities. VHF means very high frequency (VHF).

melee
A **melee** is disorganized hand-to-hand fighting at close range with little control once it starts.

micron
A micron is 1,000,000th of a meter. In filters, it measures the diameter of filter pores that block particulates and biological cells that are larger than filter pore size.

NiMH battery
A **n**ickel **m**etal **h**ydride (NiMH)chemistry is used to make a rechargeable NiMH battery.

MRE
A **m**eal **re**ady to **e**at (MRE) is a self-contained, individual ration, in plastic packaging.

MURS
The **m**ulti-**u**ser **r**adio **s**ervice (MURS) is a two-way radio service using five channels. It uses a narrow selection of VHF frequencies.

mylar
Mylar is a plastic film that has a thin layer of metal (usually aluminum) or silicon dioxide on its surface.

N95 respirators

An N95 respirator is a particulate-filtering mask respirator meeting the US National Institute for Occupational Safety and Health (NIOSH) N95 classification of air filtration. It filters at least 95% of airborne particles. It provides protection against particulates but not against gases, oils, or vapors.

N95 respirators are functionally equivalent to those regulated by non-U.S. jurisdictions, such as FFP2 respirators of the European Union and KN95 respirators of China.

nail board

A nail board is a board with nails driven through and used to impede walking areas.

NBC

A **n**uclear, **b**iological, and **c**hemical (NBC) designation indicates if an item is usable in that environment.

night vision

Night vision is the ability to see in low-light conditions using technological means. Humans have poor night vision compared to animals.

nitrile gloves

Nitrile gloves are disposable gloves used for patient examination and some procedures. They are nitrile butadiene rubber, which is puncture resistant.

nitrogen storage

Nitrogen storage is a storage method that displaces oxygen and water vapor with the inert gas nitrogen.

nominal micron rating

A nominal rating indicates ability to prevent passage of a minimum percentage of particles greater than the nominal rating's stated micron size. An example is "95% of 10 micron" – where the filter prevents 95% of all 10 micron and larger particles from passing.

NV

Night vision refers to seeing in low-light. See *night vision*.

oxidation

Oxidation occurs when oxygen reacts with a material, causing either surface or entire material reactions. It can occur slowly, as in the formation of rust, or much more rapidly, as in the case of burning fuel. The oxidation of food typically causes the food to be spoiled

oxygen permeability

Oxygen permeability is the measurement of the amount of oxygen gas that passes through a substance over a given period. It relates to the penetration of oxygen through packaging to sensitive foods and pharmaceuticals.

permethrin

Permethrin is a medication and insecticide. As a medication, applied to the skin as a cream or lotion, it is used to treat scabies and lice. As an insecticide, it can be sprayed on clothing or mosquito nets to kill the insects that touch them.

potable water

Potable water is clean enough to drink.

pool shock

Pool shock is granules of calcium hypochlorite that makes a chlorine solution that can be used to disinfect water.

pre-filtering

Pre-filtering refers to trapping the larger particles out of a liquid.

prepper

A prepper is an individual who prepares for emergencies and disasters, including possible disruptions in social or political order.

PV system

A **p**hotovoltaic (PV) system, or solar power system, generates electrical power by means of photovoltaic cells. It consists of several components, solar panels to convert sunlight into electricity, a solar inverter to convert panel output from direct to alternating current, mounting, cabling, and other accessories. As used here, it often uses an integrated battery solution to store electrical power.

quicklime

Quicklime is calcium oxide (CaO) and a widely used chemical compound. Quicklime is inexpensive and commonly available. It readily combines with water to form a plaster.

respirator

A respirator is a device that protects the wearer from inhaling hazardous atmospheres, including fumes, fumes, gases, and particulates such as dusts and airborne microorganisms.

Respirators range from inexpensive disposable masks (surgical masks) to reusable models with replaceable cartridges (gas masks).

ringer

A ringer is a chain mail like scrubbing device specifically used to clean cast iron cookware.

rocket stove

A rocket stove is an efficient stove that uses small-diameter wood fuel.

saline

Saline, also known as saline solution, is sodium chloride (salt) in water. Use it to clean wounds.

SAM splint

A **s**tructural **a**luminum **m**alleable **(SAM)** splint is a compact, lightweight device designed for immobilizing bone and soft tissue injuries.

SAME

Specific area message encoding (SAME) encodes the Emergency Alert System and NOAA Weather Radio.

scanner

A scanner is a radio receiver that tunes to two or more frequencies, simultaneously. It stops when it finds a signal on one and then scans other frequencies when the transmission ends.

scope

A scope is an optical sighting device based on a telescope. It uses a graphic image mounted in its optical system to give an aiming point.

semi-automatic

A semi-automatic firearm, called self-loading firearm (though fully automatic and selective fire firearms are technically also self-loading), is one whose action mechanism automatically loads a following round of cartridge into the chamber and prepares it for subsequent firing, but requires the shooter to manually use the trigger to fire each shot.

short-wave (SW) radio

Short wave radio is radio transmission using shortwave radio frequencies. There is no official definition of the band but the range always includes the high frequency band and generally extends from 1.7-30 MHz.

sleep system

A sleep system uses layers of sleeping bags to adjust sleeping warmth for ambient temperature.

SODIS

Solar water **dis**infection (SODIS) is a type of portable water purification that uses solar energy to make biologically contaminated (e.g., bacteria, viruses, protozoa, and worms) water safe to drink. Solar water disinfection uses heat from the sun to heat water to 158–212°F . Water containing non-biological agents such as toxic chemicals or heavy metals requires additional steps to make the water safe to drink.

solar array

A solar array is the assembly of solar panels, the visible part of the PV system. It does not include all of the other hardware. See *PV system*.

squelch (control)

The squelch adjustment limits the background noise of a radio transmission.

starlight scope

A starlight scope amplifies extremely low light, allowing the user to see at night.

Steri-strips

Steri-strips, is a brand of wound closure strips, are surgical tape strips used to close small wounds. Apply them across the wound in a way that pulls the skin on either side of the wound together. Use wound closure strips instead of sutures because they lessen scarring and are easier to keep clean.

survival knife

Survival knives are knives used for survival purposes, often in an emergency when the user has lost most of his/her main equipment.

survivalist

A survivalist is an individual who prepares for catastrophes, including disruptions in social or political order, on scales from local to international.

tang

The tang is the metal portion of a knife. Full tang refers to a single full-length piece of metal. A full tang makes the knife stronger and allows hammering by the grip butt.

tangle-foot

Tangle-foot is a low to the ground web of twine or rope that makes walking difficult and slows down walking through an area.

tanto point knife

The term derives from Japanese swords in which the point of the sword pierces armor.

tectonic plate

A tectonic plate is a massive, irregularly shaped slab of solid rock. Seismic activity often occurs where plates meet.

TEOTWAWKI

The end of the world as we know it (TEOTWAWKI)

thermal imaging

All objects with a temperature above absolute zero emit infrared radiation. The amount of radiation emitted increases with temperature. Thermography allows one to see variations in temperature. Warm objects stand out well against cooler backgrounds.

triangular bandage

It is typically made of muslin and used as a roller bandage, compression bandage, sling, tourniquet, or litter strap. Their utility makes them great for inclusion in a first aid kit.

trip wire

A trip wire is a wire or a line connected to a signal and placed in the path of objects in a specific area. The signal activates when an object loosens or breaks the trip wire.

trunked radio

A trunked radio system is an automated two-way radio system that uses a control channel to automatically direct radio traffic. It enables encrypted transmissions when it converts analog signals to digital signals.

UHF radio

Ultra high frequency (UHF) designates frequencies between 300 MHz and 3 GHz. UHF radio waves propagate mainly by line of sight. Hills and large buildings block UHF signals, although transmission through walls is strong enough for indoor reception.

VDC

Volts DC (VDC)

VHF radio

Very High Frequency uses frequencies from 30-300 MHz. Common uses for VHF are broadcasting, land mobile radio systems, and data communication.

water disinfection

Water disinfection is the process of removing or killing undesirable biological organisms, suspended solids, and gases from water.

water purification

Water purification removes undesirable chemicals and viruses from disinfected water to produce water for medical use.

weather alert radio

A weather alert radio is a specialized radio receiver designed to receive a public broadcast service, typically from government-owned radio stations, dedicated to airing weather reports on a continual basis. Routine weather reports are interrupted by emergency weather reports whenever needed. Weather radio services may also broadcast non-weather-related emergency information.

Wonderbag

A Wonderbag is a stand-alone, insulated bag designed to reduce the fuel required to cook food. The Wonderbag uses thermal insulation to continue cooking and keep food warm.

yoyo fishing reels

Yoyo fishing reels are automated fishing reels that can be unattended.

This page intentionally blank.

Appendix
Important Authors (additional reference)

John "Lofty" Wiseman (*The SAS Survival Handbook*)
Carla Emery (*Country Living*)
Joe and Amy Alton
James Wesley, Rawles
Joel Skousen
Jim Cobb
Creek Stewart
M.D. Creekmore
Max Velocity
Jeff Cooper
Peggy Layton
Dave Canterbury
Cody Lundin, with an open mind
Mel Tappan, with an occasional grain of salt
David Werner (*Where There Is No Doctor*)
Rory Miller (*Facing Violence*)
William Forgey, M.D. (*Wilderness Medicine*)
John Kallas, PhD. (*Edible Wild Plants*)
Buck Tilton and John Gookin (*NOLS Winter Camping*)
Anthonio Ackkermans (*The Complete Survival Shelters Handbook*)
Multiple Authors and Contributors (*The Special Operations Forces Medical Handbook*)
A fictional book that is especially relevant.
    William R. Fortschen (*One Second After*)

A survivalist blog that is a source of useful, non-intrusive, information, and relatively ad-free is: https://survivalblog.com.

This page intentionally blank.

Index

A

B

C

G

H

I

K

L

M

N

This page intentionally blank.

About this book and K.Z. Williams

There is a difference between being a prepper and being a survivalist. A prepper prepares for the most probable disasters while a survivalist also prepares for unlikely catastrophic events.

As a long-time prepper, I tested products that promised to solve prepping needs. Using techniques developed over years of evaluating product claims, I developed an insight into what works. I came to understand the amount of preparations overlap.

Helping companies and clients prepare for Y2K events opened my eyes to how unprepared most people were. Most companies and people do not realize that their preparations do not go far enough. This book covers cascading effects and supplies you need to have **before** stores are stripped clean. **Anticipate, don't react.**

The book uses hard lessons learned coping with floods, an earthquake, tornadoes, a long-term power outage, and a hurricane.

The first step is to understand what is probable where you live. For probable events, it became clear that wilderness skills were far less important than knowing the reality of what to expect.

Bugging out is not a realistic survival plan. Surviving in the wild is not a practical solution. Building a survival kit based on a bug-out bag ignores what you need to survive at home in a bug-in.

In this book, I guide you on how to survive and how to protect yourself, your family, and your bug-in when others want what you have.

Graphic Credits

Front cover cyber picture courtesy of Pedro Nunez Photography

Traffic jam picture (page vii) courtesy of PixaBay

Ice picture (page xi) courtesy of Blue Ridge Life

House flood (page xi) courtesy of Public Adjuster Group

Tsunami picture (page 97) courtesy of ResultsIreland.

Back cover graph courtesy of Munich RE, NatCatSERVICE

Back cover tsunami picture courtesy of ResultsIreland

Graphs courtesy of NOAA and USGS

www.ingramcontent.com/pod-product-compliance
Lightning Source LLC
Chambersburg PA
CBHW061346280526
45784CB00001B/149